Stress, Power and Ministry

John C. Harris

stress, power and ministry

An approach to the Current Dilemmas
of Pastors and Congregations

By John C. Harris

"Nothing is whole, but first it is rent."
W.B. Yeats

contents

ACKNOWLEDGMENTS

The idea of exploring in depth the leadership dilemmas of pastors came originally from a series of seminars conducted as a part of the Parish Intern Program for newly-ordained Episcopal clergypersons in the Baltimore-Washington area. These seminars surfaced special problems of stress, dependency, authority and power that confront parish pastors perhaps more acutely than at any time in recent history. A special thanks goes to Bob Mahon and Jim Adams for their work in these seminars and for what they taught me.

Developing this material into book form was directly due to the encouragement and advice of Loren Mead, Director of the Alban Institute. I particularly want to thank the Rt. Rev. William Creighton and the Rt. Rev. David Leighton for giving me the six months leave in which the first draft was written.

I owe a debt of gratitude to my colleagues, clergy and laity, who were sources of insight and learning for me, and whose courage in the face of the complexities of contemporary ministry was often inspirational.

At a very personal level I want to express great appreciation for two of my teachers. To Herbert Cohen for my own understanding of the central and positive role of anxiety in human life and of the psychodynamics of individuation and growth; for Charles Penniman, now dead, since many of my ideas about the Church's task and the need to make theological statements concrete are attributable directly to him.

Several people shaped portions of this book by their criticism and suggestions. I want to thank them: Ruth Libbey, Chris Bedford, Loren Mead, and Celia Hahn.

I am very grateful to Ruth Libbey and Rachel Lyman, who spent untold patient hours deciphering my handwriting and retyping successive manuscript drafts.

I thank Morag Simchak and Celia Hahn for carefully editing the manuscript, paring it and tightening it beyond my power to do so, and Celia Hahn for designing the cover and book layout. A great deal is owed the Alban Institute office staff who, as publication deadline drew near, worked long hours - Patti Loy and Jeanne Edwards.

I am also grateful for a small grant from the Cloud Nine Fund of the Women of St. Stephen's Church in Seattle, Washington, to assist in the production of the book.

Perhaps my greatest gratitude is to my wife Tucker and my sons Andy, Bill, and Matthew, who had to bear, as much as I, the effort involved.

Finally, to Loren Mead, my warmest appreciation. Not only was he in on the birth of this book, but the Alban Institute was adventuresome enough to publish it.

*　*　*　*　*　*

For the second edition, Moira Mathieson corrected errors discovered in the first edition, made editorial improvements and revised the format.

John C. Harris

PREFACE

In my work with Inter/Met Seminary in the early '70s, I was privileged to be an 'insider' in dozens of congregations in metropolitan Washington. I also came to know well their clergy — Protestant, Catholic, and Jewish. One of my unshakeable findings was how similar are the problems that vex the clergy and their congregations, despite economic, social, and religious differences.

After reading John Harris' book, I know much more about how my observation can be explained. A more sensitive analysis of the work and life situation of the clergy may exist, but I do not know of one. Previous studies of the clergy role tend to be restricted just to a study of the **role** itself, or what the author wants the role to be theologically or sociologically. The difference with Harris' work is that it is a study of **persons** in the role of clergy that faithfully reports the actual shape of their problems as well as solutions that are also borne out by their experience.

Today it is true, without exception in my experience, that the identity and strength of the clergy is the key to the vitality of congregational life. There was once a time when the objective fact of priesthood or rabbinate was enough to carry an individual with low self-esteem through difficult times in the tasks of leadership. Something ought to be done because "Father" or "Rabbi" or "Pastor" wanted it to be done. The role itself was so much more than the person that it overshadowed individual reality. Such is no longer the case. The personal authenticity of the minister, priest or rabbi is the greatest strength of any congregation. The inauthenticity of the clergy is the greatest weakness of organized religion.

The causes of this development are complex, rooted in modern concepts of religion and individuality. Harris' work should be seen as a counterpart to Robert Bellah's studies of modern religion or Thomas Luckman's analysis of the new relation between religion and the individual. The effect of the change in the clergy role from a 'given' social reality that submerged the person

1

to a unique form of leadership of personal transformation is to heighten vastly the stress and anxiety of the practising clergy.

The subject matter of this book is the actual life of clergy and congregations as I know them, made afraid by the great power and depth of the message and symbols carried by their faith, and made afraid by the bewildering tasks of relating their faith to modern problems. The most interesting parts of Harris' work for me were the many painstaking accounts of clergy and their congregations at work in the power of their fears or working through their fears to a more redemptive stage of life.

This book should be read by every 'search committee' charged with finding a new clergy leader. It should also be read by every clergyperson seeking new assignments. Denominational executives and those charged with helping clergy and their families will benefit from Harris' intimate knowledge of the work and emotional problems of clergy. Clergy and boards of congregations that have experienced difficulty could also benefit from a close reading, for it is likely that the roots of their problems will be discussed. Seminary educators should take every word of this book to heart.

John Harris is qualified by many years of personal experience in the pastorate, as well as distinguished service as Assistant to the Bishop of the Episcopal Diocese of Washington, with major responsibility for clergy training and development. I am personally happy to see his years of personal struggle with the issues contained in this book come to fruition as a gift to his colleagues in every denomination.

                              John C. Fletcher
              Associate for Theological Education
                    The Alban Institute, Inc.

A JUNE SUNDAY IN WASHINGTON, D.C.

It is a humid Washington summer morning. I am standing inside an early nineteenth century Episcopal Church. Around me are about two hundred worshippers who have just attended the 11 o'clock service. The church nave is a large, high-ceilinged room with white walls and coffee-brown pews. Tall, lightly-tinted windows let in the summer light. Throughout there is a feeling of roominess, of open space.

As a visitor, I am relieved to catch sight of a couple I know. The congregation is mostly white, middle-aged, with a few blacks and a sprinkling of younger couples. Interestingly, there are more men than I usually see in church. Plenty of coats and ties, print dresses and white gloves.

People exit slowly, greeting and talking. Some depart through big side doors out into the bright sun. Most of us move to the vestibule and on into a large room where coffee is served from two tables covered with white linen. Cup in hand, I move off, heading for the couple I had just seen in the crowd.

A few feet away, not far from the main door, stands the minister. He is lanky, grey-eyed, in his mid-forties. His white robe looks too heavy for the hot summer air. People approach him to talk. These exchanges vary. Some are quite personal, some with people obviously new to the church. Apart from those waiting to have a word, no one appears to take special notice of the minister.

Later on, the room empties. Coffee pots, used cups, ash trays are hustled away on metal carts. A few couples remain, deep in conversation. The minister, looking eager to go now, moves toward the vestibule doors, where almost at once he is waved down by a lingering couple who begin to talk with him energetically.

That Sunday afternoon, the minister and I sat on the porch of his house next door. He had brought drinks from the kitchen, removed his jacket, and sprawled comfortably in a big chair. As we talked over the morning, I asked why he had apparently abandoned the old custom of standing at the church door to greet people as they left.

"Several reasons," he answered slowly. "For one thing, it invites dishonesty or at least empty talk. This way people who want to see me can do so at the coffee hour in a fairly unhurried way. People who don't aren't forced to make up things to say. The worship committee suggested I stand off to one side, some place easy to see and get at. I usually stay put and don't go around greeting people. Another reason is that standing at the door acting like a party host misrepresents my function as rector. The rector is not the only person at the center of the congregation."

He had come to this church three years before from a settled southern community, replacing a man who had been pastor for thirty years. His leadership style and lack of conventional piety rapidly marked him off from his predecessor.

"There's something else." He thought for a moment. "It's harder to put into words. It has to do with what I see happening now and what I hope will happen in the future. In my last church there was little turnover. Everyone went back four and five generations. Here - well, we've added a hundred and fifty members this past year. They come because they like my style and they like what goes on. But if you look at the pin-chart in my office, you'll see they come from all over the city. They are diverse. They have different expectations of a church. Underneath, I think everyone here wants the same thing - a family. But they want it in different ways. Some press hard for an evangelistic emphasis. Some look for self-realization, personal growth. Some want to be involved in community action. And the old members want it mostly like it's been. But everybody wants a community that cares for 'them.'

"The crunch comes because our very pluralism threatens that possibility. We haven't found our identity yet."

Drawing on the experience of several nearby parishes, they had devised distinctly different ways for new people to come into the congregation and learn whether it was right for them. Groups formed around personal needs: life issues, prayer and Bible study, social action, a series of week-night conversations introducing people to the parish and its theology of Christian experience, dinner dances held in the fall and spring. Even non-participation in activities was explicitly legitimized.

"Things heat up when I don't react in expected fashion," he went on. "I work differently than my predecessor. For instance, I really try to be straight about what's going on with me. But in useful ways - I try to put my own questions and experiences into sermons. Many people aren't used to that from a minister and it unsettles them. I want to widen our concept of lay ministry inside the church, so I don't decide things and do things as he automatically would have. What counts for me is that we are straight with each other about what's going on between us, that we have some empathy for each other and for people outside the church, and that we learn to recognize that our ultimate security lies with God as opposed to this old building next door, for example.

"That involves us in some personal pain together, and people don't come here looking for that. Yet I know no other way to find meaning and value in living. I can't push too hard. But, if I get shaky and don't let our needs and troubles surface where we can talk them through, then we'll revert into politeness and a lot of organizational busyness. That's another reason I avoid the church door. It's a kind of signal that our hope lies in working it out together, and not in leaning on one individual."

INTRODUCTION

Over the past 15 years, we have become familiar with the language of crisis in connection with organized religion. Analyses of the churches' major problems are numerous. Glock and Stark point out the widespread erosion of Christian belief among mainline clergy and laity. Thomas Luckman underscores the extent to which churches have edged to the margin of industrial societies. Jeffrey Hadden summons clergy to manage more effectively their serious differences with laity on social and theological issues. Peter Berger sees churches caught between "retrenchment" (withdrawal from the issues and new perspectives of modern life) and "accommodation" (overidentification with secular values and the loss of the Biblical message).

The crisis these five sociologists describe is the same one present in the story that begins this book. It is a crisis of adaptation. To quote Constance Jacquet, "mainline churches must find some new method of involving the membership in these communities in meaningful religious and personal experiences."

Over the last two decades, I have seen a number of factors at work in the mainline Protestant congregations of the area where I live, metropolitan Washington. These factors, when taken together, form the salient element of the crisis of adaptation as I have witnessed it in Washington.

- For the past twenty years, the wider society in which our churches live has changed so swiftly that older patterns of worship, education and participation cannot be counted on to arouse and hold the commitment of new generations of worshippers.
- Older patterns of worship often fail to nurture spiritual growth or compassion for the suffering of others in the surrounding community.
- At the same time, these older worship patterns are usually very important to a cadre of

older church members who supply the church with significant leadership and money.

● Yet the future vitality of most churches in metropolitan Washington, their capacity to be regenerative, socially concerned communities, rests not with a dwindling corps of veterans, but upon their ability to attract and touch new people from each stage of life.

● To attract and touch new people requires building and maintaining an authentic pluralism of values - a pluralism that requires a parish climate of trust at the same time it invites a candid exploration of the nature of deepened spirituality.

● Individual members must find important reasons to justify the personal tensions such a climate inevitably produces, when shopping for a more placid parish environment is an easy option.

● The pastor and the congregation continually make choices whether to face or ignore their difficulties with each other and with the basic dilemmas of life.

The choices they make are crucial not only for the parish's survival, but for its integrity as a Christian community.

Indeed, the challenge of adaptation is survival. Mainline congregations have ceased to grow at a pace equal to conservative churches - and, in the case of some denominations, have fallen behind even the population growth.

To some degree, each mainline congregation in metropolitan Washington today is engaged in a protracted struggle to adapt, to survive . . . a struggle that interlinks the personal consciousness and social sensitivities of its members with the wider human community.

How well a congregation adapts is determined directly by the quality of the relationships between a church's leaders and members. And that quality of relationship in a congregation depends largely on the personal leadership style of its pastor. The more I work with clergy and congregations, the surer I am of this. In both Roman Catholic and Protestant parishes, the pastor's personal style has always been central. But today his (and now, her) personal qualities, ways of leading, knowledge and skill are not just central, they are decisive for the well-being of the local church. In the crisis of adaptation, the role of the pastor is absolutely critical.

I have written this book because, first as a pastor

and then as Staff Director of the Washington Diocese's Commission on the Ministry, I have had the opportunity both to experience and to study how important and how difficult the pastor's role of leadership is in a congregation's process of adaptation and growth.

This book presents a very definite vision of the pastor's role in that process. It is a vision and personal understanding drawn from my own frustrations and difficulties as a pastor of a mainline congregation facing the challenges of adaptation . . . and as a counselor to ministers of similar congregations.

Because it is my book, it begins with part of my story.

1. Adaptation and Leadership: Sketching the Background

I remember a story my stepfather told me, when I was a boy, of a newly-ordained Episcopal minister in his first church in a small mill town in North Carolina. Both the mill owners and the mill workers belonged to this church and attended its services. As time passed, the grievances of the workers impressed themselves heavily on the young clergyman. Eventually, when the hands struck the mill, he supported the legitimacy of their claims. Within days, the wrath of the mill owners fell upon him like crashing surf. The Diocesan Bishop summoned him and said, in effect, "Cool it or leave. There's no room there for the kind of minister you want to be."

Resisting, the minister stayed on and continued his stand. He remained through the negotiations, until the strike was settled. The mill hands had made some gains. But the minister's usefulness was over. He resigned his position and left. This was in 1938, at the tail end of the depression.

He had both conquered and lost. He needed time and a place to grasp the meaning of the battle he had just fought. In New York, at Union Seminary, Reinhold Niebuhr was teaching a new kind of social ethics, a Biblically-based, domesticated Marxism, critical of Capitalist institutions. The young minister went north to Union Seminary and sought to put the pieces together for himself.

The minister in this story was my stepfather. His telling of it impressed my boyhood imagination. There were powerful elements of life here that I barely understood - power, hate, courage, injustice, fear. And I recall it now because it is an illustration of the Church's life, of an institution caught up in the clashing personal hungers of men and women and of the fact that ministers who involve themselves wholeheartedly in this vortex risk their jobs at the same time that they honor their conscience.

Those tragic years of the thirties have passed away like a terrifying dream. Most people living today know of that time only from the recollections of parents or grandparents. But in every way it was as much a watershed time for the churches as it was for the rest of the country. It marked the end of our belief in the power of private charity and in the Church as the healer of human ills in a modern industrial state. Since then, clergy and laity have been overtaken by a continuing, often feverish quest for the meaning of Christianity and for the place of the local congregation, so long assured, in the course of daily life.

In quieter times, the unique life experience of each new generation can be roughly integrated with the older existing body of doctrine at a rate that does not jar accepted truth. But as social change speeds up, the gap between daily experience and assumed truth rapidly widens. Religious symbols, once luminous, quickly lose power to make sense of the novel, bewildering dilemmas that are everyone's lot in life. To be a church leader involved in the struggle of such times is particularly hard.

During my adolescence, these struggles barely touched my life. My stepfather had congregations first in Roslyn, Long Island, and then in Highland Park, Illinois. They were churches typical of most larger mainline parishes - middle-class, suburban, established. I think now of my experiences in youth groups and choirs, at church picnics, as warm and nurturing. Whatever else was happening to the churches in society in the late forties and early fifties, my chief recollections of church life are of good times and close friends. Only in college did I begin to encounter questions: about myself, about Christianity, about society, about the Church's place and meaning.

A freshman English instructor, Paul Barstow, had a particularly important impact on my life. Regularly, Barstow hosted a Wednesday-night get-together for students at the Alumni House. We drank beer, ate, and talked endless hours into the night about what we believed, cared about, considered true. It was an ancient ritual, a classic kind of educational awakening. Barstow was the catalyst. He challenged everything, accepted little. He pushed us in a hundred ways to consider new questions, new perspectives. My assumptions about the world, God, and myself dissolved, reformed, dissolved again, tumbled over and over into seemingly meaningless fragments. It was an absorbing, sometimes frightening experience. Returning to the dormitory on these evenings, I would take Spring Street up through the center of town. Squarely in view at the far end stood the Congregational Church, its white front often gleaming in the clear moonlight. The cold serenity of its steeple and brilliant facade contrasted sharply with my own inner turmoil. I often thought to myself, "The Church needs to provide stability and nurture, but it needs to do more. It needs to ask the sort of questions we ask around the table back at the Alumni House. It needs to arouse doubts, to criticize itself, to get people searching within themselves."

My decision to become a minister was, like most vocational choices, a mixture of complex personal factors. I think most of these stand outside the purpose of this book. But several bear directly on it, and so are worth telling.

By the start of my senior year, I had no notion of what to do with my life. I had long since given up the closest thing to a dream I had - medicine. It had dried up and vanished at the prospect of endless hours of chemistry, physics, and mathematics, for which I had little interest and probably even less aptitude. In a laboratory I was an active danger to myself and everyone around. What caught my excitement were John Miller's classes in philosophy, some fine courses in American literature and the entire field of psychology. But these pointed nowhere vocationally. Today I would have taken time to explore different kinds of work. Then I felt mostly an oppressive sense of guilt at having no direction, dismay at how my vacillation looked like so much mush beside the seemingly steady clarity with which my most respected classmates viewed their futures.

About this time, Reinhold Niebuhr, my stepfather's teacher, came to speak at the Sunday evening chapel service. Hearing Niebuhr was something akin to a flash of lightning across the night sky - momentarily he illumined for me a landscape. Niebuhr's words, as best I can recall, focused on racial justice, and particularly the inequity of segregated school systems. But what struck me most was his passionate denunciation of the detachment and complacency of the churches, his contempt for their preoccupation with individual piety. He spoke of the Church's purpose in a way that rekindled my earlier vision - as a source of human liberation from social and psychological bondage. To a senior in college with nothing to do, Niebuhr's words cleared a path and, much more, they pointed a way that commanded my respect and complete loyalty. Moreover, not only did a decision to enter seminary relieve anxiety, it permitted me the double satisfaction of moving closer to my stepfather and also doing a piece of work that was fresh, independent, badly needed. I would find a church and with it get at the basic realities of fear and love that work in the hearts of people during most of their living hours.

I went to Virginia Seminary in the Fall of 1952. The Seminary, at that time, taught a theology of "relationship." Simply described, relationship theology rejected truth as precept, principle, or moral abstraction. Truth emerged out of the deeds and relationships of people; it was palpable, something lived and done, not bloodless, ephemeral, ideal, floating detached from life. When I graduated in 1955, I took away the notion that the congregation itself is a portion of society in microcosm, an environment for personal and social transformation. I believed then, and do now, that the local church is a dynamic field of personal interaction meant to have the effect of making us more caring, more self-searching, more conscious of the riddle and mystery of life than most of us normally ever are.

My first chance to take charge of a congregation came three years later. I had worked as assistant pastor at St. Alban's Church, a large metropolitan parish on Wisconsin Avenue in Washington. I had learned a great deal, but I was getting restless. I wanted my own chance. I wanted to see what I could do.

The church was St. John's, Broad Creek, in Oxon Hill, Maryland. It was located just south of the city's growing edge, close to the banks of the Potomac. St. John's had been founded in 1692. The present church, a single room with tall side doors and a rear balcony, was built in 1766 after a fire destroyed the 1722 building. The priest I was to replace had been pastor there for twenty years, but he had divided his time between St. John's and another, larger congregation, St. Barnabas, closer to Washington.

St. John's, though small, contained distinct groups of people. At the core were Marylanders who went back five generations, descendants of farmers and wealthy landowners. Then there was a group Peter Drucker has aptly called "knowledge workers" - professionals who came to work in the government during the fifties. There were also families whose husbands and wives both worked - teachers, electricians, nurses, managers of small businesses. Last, there were numerous military families with the husband working at the Pentagon or stationed at Andrews Air Force Base.

Several weeks before I moved to Broad Creek, the Bishop asked me to his office. Near the end of our talk he said, "St. Barnabas and St. John's are high Anglo-Catholic congregations in a growing area. People moving out there need an alternative between the two. That's

your job. Build a different style - a bit looser, less
ceremony. Open it up to young families." With a youth-
ful arrogance, I felt I knew what to do and could probably do it better than anyone else. My aim was to create
a self-reflective congregational climate, open alike to
community issues and personal renewal, where power was
mutually shared by clergy and laity.

Meanwhile, the vestry at St. John's anxiously
awaited my arrival. I was the church's first full-time
rector, and my intentions were as much stage center in
their minds as in my own. At our first meeting, before I
had actually decided to go there, they had asked in many
different ways, "If you come, what will you change?" And
I had answered honestly, "Probably nothing significant.
Important changes we'll decide together." Without over-
statement, what they thought was significant and what I
thought they thought was significant were miles apart.

How far apart I did not begin to learn until the end
of my first week there. I began to come upon things that
made me uneasy. In going over financial records, for
instance, I saw that St. John's was heavily supported by
people outside the congregation, by non-members living in
the area. That struck me as demeaning. Money came from
Friday-night bingo games, a big annual fair, bake sales.
The amounts were not huge. They could be replaced and
more if each family gave $100 a year. "This church lives
off community charity," I thought. I was only dimly
aware then that these activities had another purpose
beside money, that of bringing people together. One
means of raising money caught me completely by surprise.

When I walked into the church vestibule late one
Saturday afternoon, I saw boxes of vanilla extract on a
table against the wall. Vanilla extract? Slowly it
dawned: these bottles were to be sold on Sunday, the
money turned over to the vestry. Fleetingly, I wondered
what properties this brand of extract possessed that made
it so desirable. Was it for cooking or drinking? Since
I approached everything about this new situation with
earnest self-determination and no little anxiety, I reacted with none of the humor or lightness which might
have saved us all a lot of grief in the coming months.
My immediate impulse was to pitch all the bottles into
the churchyard creek. Common sense prevailed. I left
the bottles untouched. But I was conscious that I had
come upon a way of thinking, of making do, that was alien
to me, perplexing, and for which I felt a rising contempt.

There were other things. Earlier in the week, I had
looked over the church-school curriculum. It had been
used at St. John's since time immemorial, a trusted and

reliable friend. To my eye, it was moralistic, ominous in its judgmental tone, superstitious, literalist, worse than nothing. I had almost no choice but to get rid of it speedily and as tactfully as possible. Also, I had found in the sanctuary a three-toned door-bell type gong installed behind the altar. It was to be rung during the Sanctus and prayer of consecration by an acolyte who pressed its button with his left knee. I thought its three notes sounded as though the Avon lady had come to call. The altar itself, with its dark, heavy candlesticks, looked medieval, forbidding.

All this came together in my mind. My confidence sagged. I began to feel the walls closing in. Should I have come here at all? My dreams for this parish suddenly appeared silly and hopelessly idealistic. "There's no way I can hack this stuff," I told myself. "It's got to go - fundraising, moralism, bell, vanilla extract - the whole mess." Somewhere in my thoughts flashed a piece of hoary advice familiar to every seminarian of my generation: "Make all the changes you can during the first six months while you're still in the honeymoon phase."

With wisdom like that, who can go wrong? Consulting no one, I attacked these 'symbols' of magical religion and clergy authority. First, I disconnected the gong, and stashed all but two candelabra (which I left on the altar) in the robing room. Then, on Sunday, I appeared, not in the embroidered robes the people knew and loved, but in a plain black gown, white surplice and green stole. I felt as though a great weight had been lifted from my back. I was off to a clean, fast start. These small departures, I told myself, were likely to upset some people for a short spell but, in the long run, they were no big deal.

Looking back, I am impressed by the naive presumption with which I did it. As anyone can imagine, these changes were megatonic to most of the congregation. Waves of shock rolled over the pews. Nothing was said to me. By custom, priests were seldom challenged directly and, given the fact this was our first Sunday together, nearly everyone was disarmed. But now, recalling the scene, I can see the dismay, the hurt, the anger that swirled inside that church.

As the weeks went by, I pressed harder, mesmerized by my own unwitting needs, impervious to theirs. I summarily abandoned the church-school curriculum, picked my own, and recruited almost totally new staff to teach it. I boycotted Friday-night bingo. I made no attempt to hide my scorn of a church whose members expected others to support them.

After a few polite monthly meetings, members of the

vestry began to ask pointed questions of me, and to report angry phone calls and upset parishioners. I responded with explanations, persuasion, argument. But all the while I pressed on, convinced of what I had to do. Slowly the mood of the vestry shifted. They began to attack, but on safe, peripheral issues: I wasn't calling enough; I drove a green car instead of a black one. At last, during a meeting, a young administrator from NASA suggested the vestry adopt a procedure used in his office - a work log which would record my daily activities and which would be submitted to the vestry for evaluation in advance of each meeting. I stiffened. At that moment it seemed sickeningly clear to me that we were locked in a struggle for control, one I dare not lose. I said to them, "You do that, and you can get yourselves another man." My hand was not forced, but neither did the vestry retreat.

From then on we were stalemated. The situation was terrible and disheartening. I had alienated these people in less than six months.

I came to St. John's believing that central to Christianity was the insight that fullness of life depended on one's willingness to be vulnerable to the claims and needs of others and to risk being transparent with others. I was aware of the pitfalls of total honesty and how honesty can be used as a weapon. But I believed that generally in human relationships, openness about one's own positions and needs was a redeeming fact of life. I think my war with St. John's - and I believed it to be a war - was directed against habits of mind and behavior in the congregation that looked to me as though they walled people off from each other, stifling life under the trappings of religion. I found myself in the unfortunate position of trying to attract people to my value system by attacking theirs. Only much later did I begin to see the incongruity of my behavior, the extent to which my attitude and actions had been life-killing as well. What I had done was far over-shadowed by the way I had done it, and just as importantly, by the tough, non-negotiating stance I had adopted in response to opposition. It contradicted everything I believed.

Once, during my first months, a vestry member asked me, "Would you mind if we called you Father? That's been our custom." I hemmed a bit and replied, "I want people to call me what makes them most comfortable." In fact, I felt uneasy being called Father. It seemed to me to introduce a false distance between a clergyperson and congregation, a convenient distance which did not permit them to deal with each other as persons, only as roles. But I didn't know how to say this plausibly or convincingly, so I fudged my answer.

Yet I failed to see an important question which lay behind this parishioner's words: namely, would I allow them to be dependent on me for the authority and leadership they had counted on from my predecessor? Would I take their customs and needs seriously? The truth was that their dependency frightened me and my own confusion about how to handle it frightened me even more. I was afraid that if I surrendered ground on questions of control and authority, I would convey inconsistency and weakness, and slowly lose whatever influence I had. We would end up repeating the old pattern of St. John's - the priest high on a pedestal, passive laity, magical religion, and empty, formalized relationships.

This congregation, like many others, was afraid of change, afraid of questions dealing with the uncertainties of human life. They wanted answers, craved reassurance. I did not know then that this lay person spoke out of real fear, seeking for stability in his own need for certainty. I did not see that my own actions had been based on my fears and had made their fears more unbearable.

I was dealing with fear - my own and that of my parishioners. And I acted as though I were dealing with bells and parish calling, vanilla extract and bingo, and the struggle for power that they implied.

The people at Broad Creek, like most of us, have a constant companion in their fear. Every shift in the familiar brings at least subliminal knowledge of a reality that shadows each day: all people die. We live, but we live vulnerable to injury, disease, misfortune, loss, aging, and finally, death. In its rawest form, our knowledge and anticipation of these events can arouse profound terror. I say "can" because early in life we learn a variety of ways in which to shut out this terror. But the dread remains at our core and it is rooted in the fact that we are creatures - small, finite, and out of control of the cosmos, yet totally vulnerable within it.

Even as we mature, our anxiety is seldom direct. It is more like a voice whispering to us that our life may be meaningless, that God himself may not care for us any more than he did for the dinosaurs, that in the end we are obliterated. All things - youth, strength, talent, achievement, love - all are swept into nothingness beyond human voice or touch. [1] Our character has little tolerance for this terror. It has been the message of all great religions, and in recent years of psychoanalysis, that most of us expend tremendous energy walling off our fear, shielding ourselves against vulnerability in any form while investing someone or something external to ourselves - our passions, our wealth, our status, the state, our physical vitality, our analyst, our family, God - with the power to protect us from pain and death. So most of us may be said to live fear-determined lives in this respect. Is there a serious problem with this? I believe so. The walls that block out the terror block off at the same time our capacities to love and enter into life: to be trusting, open to others, spontaneously joyful, alive to beauty, courageous, generous, feeling delight at the wonder of life itself. That is the problem: to fend off terror successfully is to deaden ourselves to life.

In the beginning, the congregation at St. John's and I were blocked from real life with one another by our fears and prejudices against one another. There was no hope for us to find life so long as we were afraid to go into the depths of our life - which meant touching our fear, realizing its power.

In the two years after seminary and before coming to St. John's, I had consciously searched for a way, a method to help the church become the kind of vital community I have described earlier in this chapter. But there wasn't any method; the seminaries did not teach one. In other churches, I saw pastors and laity struggling with the same question: was there some form of education or organization that would help us get below the surface of life with each other?

One day, Bill Baxter, then rector of St. Mark's Church on Capitol Hill, called to invite me to meet with a man from St. Louis who had a new slant on parish adult education. He was Dr. Charles Penniman and his method was a reversal of the traditional approach of taking religious precepts and applying them to life. In Penniman's view, the teacher helps people examine the critical places where life is under stress. Then by a series of deepening stages he or she explores with them the basis on which they make decisions and the consequences of these ways for their lives. Throughout, the symbols of the Church and its lore are used to illumine human life and to interpret the actual experience the class has together. People may decide to change or not. Simply, Penniman wanted to take the priest out of the driver's seat as an answer-giver and put him or her in a position to set the conditions for spiritual search, to tie that search closely with the struggle, pressures, anxieties everyone meets as part of the hazardous enterprise of living.

At St. John's I began holding adult classes that drew upon Penniman's insights. The congregation had grown in size, chiefly because the area around was grow-

ing. It was these new people who responded most grate-
fully to the adult classes. Many said they wished to
talk about their families, their work, their personal
quandaries, but they wanted to do it in a setting where
there was competent leadership, care, and a desire to
find a meaningful direction for living. They were hungry
for such experience and, in varying degrees, the adult
classes began to prove it.

In part because of the success of the adult classes,
new people who came to St. John's stayed. The congregation achieved self-sufficiency after two and a half
years.

New people and solvency eased some of the past pain.
And I found myself feeling strong affection for many of
the older members of the church. Still, there was uneas-
iness in the air and, while there were many issues that
fueled the tension, they all came down in the end to one
issue: my leadership.

At St. John's, the fear of change on the part of the
leaders of the congregation was persistently expressed as
a wish for directive leadership from me. My values
favored a shared ministry - a more equal distribution of
influence between clergy and laity. The vestry at St.
John's were never quite comfortable with this.

An example. Wine and beer had traditionally been
served at church gatherings off church property. But
feelings clashed when it came to serving alcohol in any
form in the parish hall. The vestry at my insistence
debated the question at length. The vote was, as I
recall, one for, one against, and eight abstentions. One
message to me was clear. They thought a good minister
should have decided the matter himself. If he wouldn't
do that, then he shouldn't let the issue come up in the
first place. By encouraging the question, many thought I
was causing dissent and trouble.

One member of the congregation put it this way.
"Father Harris, let me tell you what I think the priest's
job is. The priest's job is to teach people the truth.
What people need to hear is the teaching of Jesus -
what's right and what's wrong. Your job is to teach
that." On the other hand, directive leadership on my
part was often equally unacceptable. Against the tide of
this ambivalence, my determined efforts to shift the
character of St. John's ministry to one of joint sharing,
especially given my own unsureness and rigidity, made me
appear uncompromising and unapproachable. Undoubtedly,
at times, I was.

It took close to five years for me to achieve a
better fit between my own teaching and my actual leadership behavior. A lot of things went into the change. I

had to feel secure enough to listen to what was being said to me, to accept feedback. I had to learn to appreciate the slowness with which people and institutions grow. I had to learn to press home important questions about our mutual life together, but without condemnation. Somehow, we made it through together. The classes helped. My own growth helped. And simple kindness and willingness to stick at it on the part of many people probably helped most of all. Even so, the tension was never absent. The struggle was always there.

Pastors in my situation, not uncommon today in mainline congregations, are in a delicate position. Their reactions to the congregation's view about shared leadership are critical. Almost without exception, their response forces an adaptation of the traditional view of the pastor's role. Like most adaptations, this search for a new accommodation is stressful. On the one hand, strong disappointment and anger at their leadership style will likely interrupt the pastor's ability to work well with an important part of the parish leadership. On the other hand, the reactions of the parish may reflect a serious (though well-intended) effort to defend themselves against anxiety created by exchanges and disagreements on key matters which threaten the equilibrium of the congregation.

Depending on the situation in the parish at the moment, any request to reassert more direct control may be appropriate or not. Either way, the pastor's response carries super-important weight for the congregation.

To make such a decision well, pastors need to have the personal strength to tolerate the stress of disappointing key individuals, and must have sufficient diagnostic skill to read accurately the state of the parish. They need to interpret their actions non-defensively. In particular, they must have a reasonably clear picture of the core task of congregational life. Much of this I did not possess, except in rudimentary degree, and in the seminary I had never been taught the first thing about the political arts of parish leadership.

I see five basic tasks for a pastor today:
- awakening in people awareness of the mystery and dependability of God;
- enabling people to grapple with fear: fear of growth, fear of living, fear of others, fear of oneself, fear of suffering and death;
- focusing the individual's search for meaning so that it connects directly with the daily circumstances of life;
- fostering self-sanity: less self-deception, for example, about one's own needs and more realism

about the limited ability of human beings and human institutions to satisfy them;
- engendering compassion: a capacity for empathy with the hopes and sufferings of others.

These goals or tasks are not new, but the pastor's situation in mainline denominations is new. It is a delicate state of affairs in which personal factors between pastor and members rule the internal climate of parish life, mold the parish's response to its environment, and determine what tasks the congregation can seriously accept as basic. The pastor's authority evolves, not from canonical law or religious belief, as it did fifty years ago, but much more from a reciprocal understanding with the laity about the task of the Church and the framework of expectations in which both will work together.

Given the voluntary nature of churches, it is a situation which continuously challenges the pastor to make judgments between conflicting rights. If the congregation is to adapt, the pastor must risk alienation by allowing, sometimes stimulating, the tension-producing processes of self-examination and self-discovery. Yet a pastor who becomes alienated from a significant number of members cannot communicate effectively, and a pastor unable or unwilling to risk disappointment or anger deprives the congregation of the leadership it requires to be a viable Christian community in today's world.

This tension is inescapable for every parish today. Indeed, it is a tension which involves the core lay leaders as well. Perhaps all this is obvious, but the implications of this new situation for clergy and churches are not widely understood or recognized.

We need to become far more conscious of this tension. We need a perspective that explains how a pastor and congregation build effective relationships that are self-examining, mutually supportive and risk-taking. We need methods of education and teaching that supply theological guidelines, psychological knowledge and organizational skills that pastors and churches require. We do not have them in hand as yet. This is the frontier and we have just started to push it back.

What concerns me most is that this new situation has largely caught us unawares. With painful frequency, pastors grapple with the problems of leadership in ways that rob them of fulfillment in their vocations and block their effectiveness. The fact is that a cluster of serious, often covert institutional and social factors weigh heavily on the pastors' capacity to lead. Only as they recognize these special factors, realize their impact on them personally, and develop counter measures, can they sustain their balance as effective congregational leaders.

There is a choice ahead for mainline congregations: it is whether or not their own internal and public policies will express the ancient message of the Gospel that grace is possible for us only as we allow ourselves to be morally vulnerable to the complex world of human relationships.

As in the parable of the Last Judgment in Matthew, to allow oneself to be moved and claimed by the hungry and poor is to become interlinked with the human world and to be blessed. Churches must choose whether to offer their members detachment from the moral claims of the human community, or to summon them to something altogether different: a serious quest for new communal forms that both nourish our personal selves and arouse in us a consciousness of our common bond with all who press forward toward a public world of generosity and justice.

Clergy and lay leaders who seek ways to minister to traditional congregations in these circumstances confront difficult elements - institutionally and socially - which resist their intentions. Authentic parish leadership, I believe, hinges on learning what these elements are and seeking answers to what is involved in their mastery.

In Oxon Hill, a group of lay people and I began as frightened adversaries, blocked in our ability to help each other by our fears, our ignorance of the forces pressing in on us, and our lack of clarity about how or where to move. We did the best we knew, and there was pain and fulfillment.

In the years since, I have worked at understanding those difficult but critical interactions by which the pastor leads in collaboration with his or her people, and by which both, together, face the fear of change. In that process, the pastor has a special and very difficult role to play.

It was the role my stepfather attempted in North Carolina; it was the role I attempted in Oxon Hill; it is the role countless other pastors are attempting daily in thousands of congregations.

2. The Dilemma Within Congregational Life

> He is the Truth.
> Seek Him in the kingdom of anxiety.
> You will come to a great city that has
> expected your return for years.
>
> W. H. Auden

In the summer of 1975, **The Washington Post** published a story titled "White Church's Walls Tumble." [1] For years, Emmanuel Episcopal Church had been an all-white congregation in an area populated almost entirely by blacks. The members of Emmanuel lived elsewhere - in Virginia and Maryland, some as far as fifty miles away. Each Sunday, they drove back to Emmanuel as they had for decades, since before the neighborhood "turned." They came to celebrate mass, to talk, to meet together - to keep their church alive. Then, each Sunday afternoon they drove away. And from Monday through Saturday Emmanuel stood locked and shuttered against the alien black world outside.

Nearby was St. Philip's, a flourishing black Episcopal parish that had outgrown its small plant. Repeatedly, the people of St. Philip's asked to use Emmanuel's parish hall for programs and classes. The people of Emmanuel always said, "No." Then one Sunday in July, eighty-five members of St. Philip's went around the corner to Emmanuel, walked up the steps, in the door, and attended mass. Twenty joined Emmanuel and from that day they carried on a steady drum roll of insistence that Emmanuel pay attention to the community of Anacostia. The people of Emmanuel felt deeply violated. The church's solidarity was destroyed - its walls crumbled. One of Emmanuel's leaders summed up their anguish:

> The older people get, the more they dislike a change, and they will resist it, if for no other reason than they don't want the change. I use the word change in relation to our church - having black people coming into the community, coming to your

worship service without your consent. . . . People
seek an anchor in the face of change. I need - and
I think a lot of people in this world do - something
that is steady, with all the changes going on. You
need a solid rock some place, and to me personally,
the tradition and the service at Emmanuel provided
that. [2]
In any discussion of this story, we would find
ourselves talking of racism, of the absence of compassion, of calculated indifference, of the worst aspects
of cultism. But, I wonder if my readers can see something of themselves in the words I have just quoted. In
asking that question, I have no wish to create special
sympathy for Emmanuel's members. But if we can see
something of ourselves in them, we shall come face to
face with a powerful emotion that engulfs us all and
dominates the affairs of denominations and churches from
Boston to Los Angeles, from Seattle to Atlanta. This
emotion is a hunger for stability, for a whole unified
life in a world "where everything seems to be coming
loose."
When we think of crisis in the churches now, we
think, for example, of Episcopalians at war over women's
ordination and the new Prayer Book, or Lutherans battling
over a liberal seminary, or Roman Catholics bitterly
divided about abortion and clerical celibacy. But these
are only symptoms - troubling and vexing, to be sure, but
symptoms. The trouble with our churches goes much deeper. We are in a dilemma which we often do not even
grasp; it vitiates both clergy and lay leadership. It
is, I believe, the core difficulty in our church life,
and it springs from our unwillingness to face up to the
need for change in a rapidly changing society.
Warren Bennis, a man who has thought deeply about
how institutions cope with change, wrote:
The management of change is always a function of the way we think about and conceive the
problem. . . . We need to make an important distinction between the specific strategies ultimately
applied to the problem of change and the governing
framework, the controlling imagination, which . . .
guides the choice of these strategies. [3]
In other words, what we do as individuals about
change is, ultimately, a result of what we believe inside
about ourselves, about life, and about the world in which
we live. Answers to the problems of change do not lie
outside ourselves in the external world as much as they
do inside us, in our imaginations and our souls. We are
responsible for what we do in the face of change and what
we do is the result of what we believe - a matter of

faith. The basic emotion around change at Emmanuel was obviously fear, the controlling imagination was one of "sanctuary," the strategies employed were those of control - avoidance and withdrawal - and the end result was human isolation and, eventually organizational collapse. What collapsed as well for Emmanuel was the myth that stability lay in the power of man-made religious structures to provide safety from the impermanent nature of life.

Messiah Church

Some time back, the pastor of Messiah Church, an able, respected man in his mid-fifties, called to talk with me about his church. Messiah was a large suburban parish with a reputation for vigorous lay leadership and community-mindedness. He told me, over the phone, that he was troubled about Messiah - the leadership had grown fatigued and apathetic, the congregation felt rudderless, and he was depressed by the failure of his own efforts to improve things. We met several days later and I asked him to chronicle Messiah's recent history as he saw it.

Typical of mainline churches in the United States, the 1950s had been Messiah's salad days, a time of lush institutional growth. Membership rolls at Messiah rocketed in a few short years from several hundred to nearly two thousand. The parish developed a family-oriented program, a huge children's Sunday School, parents' classes, a sprawl of vigorous teenage groups, two-week summer camps. Pews were full and people enthusiastically invested themselves in Messiah's organizational activities. Cash flow became as predictable as the sun.

By 1960, Messiah completed a large building program. Structurally, the architect's plan reflected a belief in the continuing vitality of traditional patterns of worship and education. Amortizing the mortgage sucked up a significant part of the church's income. But not to worry - as long as the enthusiasm stayed high and the growth kept on - which no one seemed to doubt. Then, throughout America, in the early sixties, the religious "boom" waned. Messiah's records show that in 1961 member growth peaked, held in 1962, and then slowly started downhill. In 1965, the present pastor came to Messiah - just when everyone began to notice that something had gone wrong.

Throughout the sixties Messiah, like most churches, was storm-tossed by a turbulent social environment: the controversial war in Southeast Asia, the battle for racial justice at home, a ballooning population of people under thirty, increasing street crime, new life patterns and a deepening erosion of family life, people on the move from job to job or city to city, growing antagonism toward the government, women's search for a new place, and everywhere kids and drugs.

Closer at hand, Messiah's neighborhood changed. High-rise apartments shoved aside the small businesses and little shops east of the church. In nearby residential areas, elderly couples sold out to younger, affluent parents eager to find roomy houses at decent cost and schools free from black children. By 1970, the state university opened an extension nearby, drawing large numbers of commuting students. In 1972, less than two blocks away from Messiah a center for Transcendental Meditation began a land-office business.

Messiah's vitality had ebbed. The parish experienced problems widely shared by churches in the sixties and seventies. The church school shrank to one quarter of its 1961 size. The youth program died. Membership bottomed out at around 800 in 1971. Even one bright spot - a steady increase in giving by a declining membership - was rapidly erased by inflated maintenance costs that zoomed up from 6% to 20% a year. But most significantly, Messiah did not draw fresh members from the new waves of people flowing into the area; it made no contact at all with the college. A shift had occurred, too, in Messiah's atmosphere. The spirit and excitement of the past were gone. In their place had grown a kind of malaise, mingled with nostalgia, a flaccid amicability with little interest in new initiatives. This, more than any other symptoms of Messiah's trouble, alarmed its pastor.

What went on behind the scenes during all of this? Messiah had a tradition of alert managerial leadership and a pride in working with high organizational efficiency. When the lay leaders and pastor at Messiah finally saw the danger signals, they set to work energetically to reverse the decline.

* From 1966-1974 the church organizational structure was overhauled five times by lay leaders with considerable knowledge of administration.
* Each May the church board held a two-day goal-setting retreat to organize for the coming year.
* A series of young assistant ministers was hired to pump life into the flagging youth program.
* New formats for Sunday-morning worship were regularly tried out, including guitar masses and all the trial services from the proposed new Episcopal Prayer Book.
* Consultants were called in to help revise the church school curriculum from top to bottom nearly every year.

* A family-calling program was inaugurated.
* A program of house communions and bible-study groups blossomed, then inexplicably petered out.
* The adult education commission tried different patterns of adult classes, which were moderately well attended.
* Annually, the board spawned new program ideas, recruited leaders, founded new commissions, until at length it presided over a maze of activity that was nearly impossible to track, support, or comprehend.

Because Messiah's congregation had a large number of professional managers, these strategies were generally well planned and well promoted. Yet for all this persistent effort, Messiah failed to recover its vitality. More and more, program activity, recruitment of leaders, committee management and budget debates consumed the board's energy. Board meetings grew longer, until eventually the same sense of hopelessness felt by the pastor spread out into the board.

What had gone wrong?

Messiah's leaders were dominated by fear and it destroyed their capacity to be a vital, problem-solving, truth-seeking community of people. There were fears of personal criticism, of fiscal collapse, of the growing religious pluralism among the members, of younger members taking over, of giving up a trusted administrative formula, of failure. Perhaps the nature of these fears is not as important as the effect of their presence, for it is probably more accurate to say that Messiah was dominated by fear of strong emotion - of the creative excitement and intense anxiety that would break loose if people started saying what was truly on their minds, or asking questions, or opening up differences, or listening to each other's wishes and dreams, or acknowledging how badly they felt about the way things were going and facing the harsh realities of their situation.

Messiah's leaders had much to fear. They faced serious problems of adaptation. Messiah's leaders were not paralyzed by problems, but by the fear of the anxiety they would feel if they faced them.

At one point, Messiah's pastor told me a story that illustrated how powerful and life-destroying this fear was. At a board retreat several years before, a memorable exchange occurred. As the retreat began, one member spoke up and said, "In addition to setting goals for next year, I wonder if we could talk over how we feel about the way board meetings go. I've got some thoughts, and probably others do, too. Can we save some time for that?" Silence descended like a pall over the room. Then a senior lay official turned to the speaker and, in a lightly bantering tone, skewered him to the wall: "Great idea, Harry. We can all get on our couches, do touchie-feelies, and stare at our navels. You can lead us, how about it?" Harry's feeble protest was swallowed up in the uneasy laughter that followed. The subject was never raised again.

There is another important aspect to this story. It shows how Messiah's leaders neatly reinforced each other in an unwitting but powerful collusion to avoid the emotional side of parish life.

The lay leaders at Messiah carried into church relationships standards of behavior, developed in their home and work settings, that highly valued rationality, objectivity, politeness, and staying cool under stress. The pastor, in turn, though a competent administrator and religious leader with a delightful wit, was very difficult to know. After a time, I came to see him as a highly protected individual, cautious and guarded, whose life struggles were hidden from his congregation and who found it hard to express empathy or irritation directly. People kept their distance from him, a state of affairs he seemed to prefer. He gave the impression of a man closed to new possibilities in himself and in others, a man who had stopped learning. His fears and guarded manner worked hand in glove with the non-self-examining stance of Messiah's leaders. The mix was a perfect recipe for stagnation.

Interestingly, during our meetings he became increasingly self-disclosing, candid about his work frustrations, troubles in his marriage, his fears about his career. But in coming to me he was really looking for a "better mousetrap," a safe programmatic strategy for revitalizing Messiah. As we came to trust each other, we talked about how he had contributed to Messiah's trouble. He began to see, intellectually at least, something of his own role and the board's in depersonalizing relationships in the church. He recognized that if things were to improve he had to decide whether he wanted to change his style, thus opening up difficult questions about Messiah's mission, inviting feedback, examining relationships and norms of behavior, going on the line about his own personal reactions. In the end, he rejected the path I proposed. He was right, at least in this sense - that the congregational self-study I advocated would not have been useful if he were not personally committed to it and ready to take personal risks as well.

Messiah's controlling image was "bureaucracy." Change in all forms was frightening because it was unpredictable and potentially divisive. Stability was sought in tight rational management that placed control in as few hands as possible. The organizational charts at Messiah were held onto like little amulets. In these charts were order, safety, and clarity; they were the leadership's sacred defense against change. Messiah's dilemma lay in the fact that the more it defended itself against the human side of parish life, the more isolated the leadership became from the community and the more impersonal became the quality of the church's internal life.

This spiritual commitment to smooth bureaucratic functioning led to false assumptions about reality which doomed from the start Messiah's strategies to cope with change. **The board members focused all energy inward.** Under the amulets' spell, they repeatedly reorganized and tinkered with structure. Their eyes were closed to Messiah's community environment at a time when the main opportunities Messiah encountered came from the outside.

Three distinct groups had migrated into Messiah's sphere of influence in less than a decade: young families, young single apartment-dwellers, commuting students. For several years these groups quietly "checked out" Messiah. A new couple or individual would attend church once or twice, converse with members, perhaps be put on a "new attenders" list and get a clergy house-visit. Then one Sunday they would be gone. Why? Messiah's leaders did not ask; they did not care to know. They could well have shifted attention from the center to the boundary of the congregation, to that invisible territory between the parish and the world, where new people test the reality of the parish's identity by giving and receiving messages, finally deciding to join or leave.

True, Messiah's patterns of worship and education did not exactly reflect the values or concerns of this wave of new arrivals, but no structure existed to learn directly from the new people what they cared about, thought, expected from a church or how Messiah had meaning for them. Consequently, a prolonged series of turn-off transactions occurred between the parish and many curious, searching people - a fact which was only dimly understood, and remained unexamined.

A second false perception induced by Messiah's faith in bureaucratic stability was belief that **program production was the right remedy for every congregational ill.** One example: when church school enrollments fell drastically two years in a row, the education commission set about producing a new curriculum based on their judgment that curriculum was the problem. Overlooked were a host of other pertinent factors: communication patterns between teachers, parents and children, teacher recruitment and training procedures, basic attitudes of the children toward the church school, and the crowded format of Sunday mornings.

Messiah's lay board prided itself on planning efficiency. Yet planning efforts at Messiah persistently omitted an essential ingredient of good planning - learning what the problems were and the likely impediments to change. At all levels of Messiah's life, committees would set goals, often clear and challenging ones. But the human and organizational barriers to achieving these objectives were rarely singled out and identified. With knee-jerk regularity, committee members jumped from talk about what was needed straight into program development. The consequences were disastrous. As one member commented to the pastor, "There is no longer any relationship between energy and results. We put hundreds of hours into that new curriculum. Nothing's changed." Once again, pressure for smooth program success determined the board's behavior.

At length, people withdrew emotionally from committee work; recruitment of leaders became a constant irritating task, disappointment and impotence replaced the optimism of previous years. To combat their own growing sense of fear, Messiah's leaders sought refuge in problems of budgeting. Here was familiar ground, real control, tested knowledge. Sadly enough, here too was self-imposed isolation and deeper unreality.

Yet both the board's failure to notice Messiah's environment and a quasi-magical belief in the curative powers of program production were minor problems compared to a third assumption tacitly accepted by the majority of Messiah's leaders: **that evaluation was a waste of time.** The clergy did not seek feedback on their work; committee meetings were not critiqued; education program participants did not give their assessment of classes; members were not formally helped to articulate the differences between what they sought in their worship and what they actually got. Politeness, unexamined relationships, avoidance of life concerns - all were the order of the day. The cumulative effect of this atmosphere was to trivialize what was done, to put distance between people, to avoid authentic caring relationships; to foster insensitive decisions instead of humane policies; to deaden imagination rather than spark its creative flowering.

In point of fact, Messiah's leaders did not feel any real value in the symbols of God's permanence and dependability to which they gave intellectual assent on Sunday mornings. Their true feelings found safety in bureaucratic routine. Thus, they had neither the closeness to the members nor the information about their lives required to grapple with a changing community outside and an increasingly barren quality of life within. Control of Messiah's destiny was nearly out of their hands. Messiah had become less a human community than a physical organism - something like a dinosaur encased in a shell of biological necessity, maladaptive, lumbering into decline, its brain center programmed by past precedent and unexamined instinct.

Perhaps Messiah's story will shed light on the dilemma facing mainline churches everywhere.

The operative power of faith is the keystone in the Church's dilemma. Religious faith, whatever its form (whether Christian, Judaic, Buddhist, Hindu, etc.) must attract our assent. Contrary to the beliefs of many church leaders and pastors, it cannot be coerced or even learned. Faith must **attract** us, if we are to give ourselves over to its meaning and if its symbols are to live inside us with power. It must attract us in a particular form - as a really credible way of viewing oneself in relation to reality; it must readily shed light on the day-to-day situations of our lives; it must provide guidelines for the nature of human responsibility in the daily dilemmas of life and it must interpret how the stages of our lives may be lived out with creativity, humanity, and courage. At its fullest, faith will, to use John MacMurray's words, "draw to itself the whole current of our emotional life and release it in a flood of joyful activity." [4] So the operative effect of religious faith is to integrate the individual within himself or herself and with the human world in such a way that we believe in the basic goodness of life, believe in ourselves, and believe in one another. We stand, I believe, in the full rising tide of a process that began with the breakup of the Medieval age - the slow erosion of credible Christian claims to interpret the meaning of every aspect of life. We are not less religious than in the past. But as sociologists like Thomas Luckman and Peter Berger tell us, it is closer to our actual situation to say that we are overwhelmed by religious choices. We live in what Luckman aptly calls a "meaning cafeteria" in which religious attractions catered through a variety of sources "compete noisily for our attention" [5] - est, the Rev. Mr. Moon, astrology, psychotherapy, secular humanism, Marxism, occultism, imported forms of Eastern mysticism, plus Christianity and Judaism represented in a host of new guises, to name only a few. Individuals today must do a tremendous amount of inner synthesizing of values by themselves.

In a 1976 issue of the **Washington Post** there were some comments about life in our city:

More than half of us live in a different home

than . . . five years ago, . . . one out of four wasn't in the area then . . . . There are more than twice as many divorced people here than . . . in 1960. At least one of four children here under 18 have parents widowed, divorced, or separated . . . more than one out of five of us is living alone . . . in the town houses, condominiums, apartments and single-family houses that make up our neighborhoods . . . fewer younger women marry and . . . 50% of the women here now have jobs. [6]

Behind these figures is a sober fact: the nomadic existence of our lives means that people leave behind networks of support (friends, family, clergy, teachers, relatives) and enter new cities as strangers without ties where the re-creation of community is a delicate, problematic business. To a far greater extent than in past centuries, people are left to their own devices and with dwindling resources to make sense out of life and to live it with zest rather than fear and depression.

One might expect mainline churches like Messiah to be flooded by people seeking community, hope, and a practical faith of depth and power. Some are - such as the conservative, evangelical churches within mainline denominations. Most are not. Because along with urban rootlessness there also comes a serious questioning of traditional values, and a declining conviction of the importance of personal struggle in making things work - one's marriage, one's job, one's relationships.

One defense against the pain and emptiness of lost community ties is to make no emotional investment of any kind, not to care. It is to make "quitting" a spiritual style. So perhaps it is not altogether correct to say that we have lost a common faith and are left to our own devices to choose from among many the one that fits us best. It may be more useful to church leaders and more nearly accurate to say that there are increasing numbers of people who have lost faith in faith itself and there are many others who, seeking community and hope, no longer look to the church on the corner to share their concern.

To survive, and how best to survive - that is one horn of the churches' dilemma.

The struggle to survive involves something more perilous than stress for a pastor and a parish. It involves the temptation to "sell" Christianity in ways that people find attractive but which do not help them grapple with reality, society, or themselves. Surviving, among other things, means getting people's attention and risking one's integrity in the process.

Churches must offer credible testimony that life is

basically important and good and that there is value in working with others to make society more humane. But pastors and lay leaders, like store merchants and car dealers, are now sellers in the market place. To a significant degree, churches must remain sensitive to "consumer" preference, to the needs and preferences of private individuals. So there is always pressure to alter the nature of Christianity sufficiently to attract a broad enough base of devout followers.

Authoritarian religion is the **ne plus ultra** of this temptation. Here the congregation's leaders create a version of the Gospel appealing to our hunger for certainty and belonging. They say to us, "In a relativist world where values constantly shift, join with us, set your confusion aside. We will tell you God's will, what's right and what's wrong for you. No longer do you need to feel doubt or anxiety." In the classic manner of many religious bodies, authoritarian churches appeal to our fear but offer a spurious answer, one which reinforces helplessness and deadens our capacities to make moral judgments and take responsibility for our decisions in life.

The other horn of this dilemma stems from the power of fear in human life and constitutes a perpetual problem for Christianity. Most of us, inside ourselves, are complex battlegrounds of longing and fear. John Mac-Murray describes this basic warfare in us as well as anyone:

> There are two, and I think only two, emotional attitudes through which human life can be radically determined. They are love and fear. Love is the positive principle of life, while fear is the death principle in us. I mean that literally; and would go on to explain it by saying that you can divide men and women most fundamentally into two classes - those who are fear-determined and those who are love-determined. The former are not merely dead souls; they stand for death against life. They obstruct and fight life wherever they find it. They are the people of whom D.H. Lawrence - who understood these things better than any other man of our time - said that they are sunless. They have no sun in themselves, and they go about putting out the sun in other people. They are people of whom Jesus said that they needed to be reborn. Whereas the love-determined people have life in them, abundant life, and they turn towards life and fight for life against the forces of death. [7]

This profoundly impressive statement needs some clarification.

There are great numbers of people for whom the battle between love and fear is a conscious, daily occurrence. There are people who, if they came into their twenties or thirties as primarily fear-determined, have chosen to become as love-determined as possible. That is, they have learned to struggle against fear and for life. They are concerned to be open to their own growth and in lively interaction with people around them - spouse, children, friends, fellow workers, neighbors, public institutions. Given this kind of qualification, MacMurray's statement is an extraordinary foundation to what I want to say next.

To appreciate this other horn of the dilemma we must sense clearly just how destructive fear is, and how completely unnatural it is for us to be able to face fear directly. Affection and love by their nature stir us into active interaction with the world around us. They are powerful emotional forces that express themselves in actions of reaching out, of openness, of compassion, of challenging bad traditions, of persisting in the face of obstacles, of imagining, of being alive to the human world in which we move. Fear is the great destructive force in us. Fear shuts down spontaneity, and most importantly turns us away from others and in upon ourselves. Fear drowns out our capacities for life.

The stories of Messiah Church and Emmanuel Church amply demonstrate the destructive power of fear. The more successful we are in shutting out fear, the less we experience life, and the more frustrated we are in finding what we crave most - closeness, joy, peace, justice, community, integrity. The crowning irony, as MacMurray notes, is that fear makes us afraid of life itself, [8], afraid of the intensity living brings with it. If fear persists in us long enough, we often come to a terrible moment of recognition, perhaps in middle life or later, that life has passed us by, that we have never really lived the life given to us.

Like all religions, Christianity promises liberation from the power of fear. But unlike many religions, Christianity says the way goes against our natural instincts. There is only one way we can be released from the power of fear and that is by not avoiding it, by refusing to evade its presence in us. Here is the other side of the Church's dilemma: **its very message threatens its survival as an institution.**

The Gospel summons frightened people to embrace what they fear most, fear itself, and says that in doing so, they will find the gateway to life. When Jesus says, "In the world you shall have tribulation, but be of good cheer, I have overcome the world," he is not saying,

"Relax, faith will exempt you from suffering or misfortune or death." He is saying, quite plainly, that all these things happen to each of us - eventually and inevitably - regardless of our wishes or beliefs. Jesus is saying that when they do happen they are not to be feared. He means that in those times when the worst happens, there is present what Tillich calls "the saving possibility" - grace which brings the strength to face what is otherwise unbearable, a critical self-insight that awakens understanding, a fresh option which opens a new direction. In operative terms, the message is: you can expect misfortune, you can expect to be afraid, you can count on anxiety. If you are truly alive, and if you accept the fear and do not avoid it, it will lose its power to destroy your life.

Jesus' words are an invitation to trust, not that God will save you from the evils of life, but from the fear of them.

The Church's mission is to enable people to live with greater wholeness and trust - that is the basis of authentic stability. To do this, congregations must help their members understand fully the nature of their fears and to recognize the true viciousness of fear in destroying life. But this course threatens institutional survival. Facing fear arouses fear.

So here is the dilemma with which we must contend. On the one hand, churches are caught in a highly competitive religious market. This tempts religious leaders to pack their messages in ways that attract people by exploiting their wishes for authority and safety, thus reinforcing their fear of fear. On the other hand, if church leaders present their message as standing for spiritual growth against certainty of belief, for self-examination against complacency, for celebration and sorrow against non-feeling, for the spirit of facing fear against the spirit of protection, then the fear of the intensity of these emotions may itself frighten people away from their doors.

Is there a way through the dilemma I have described? I believe so. There are churches, individual congregations and pastors, who have pushed beyond the churches' dilemma into relationships of rebirth and courage. They have common elements worth noting, which will be discussed in the following chapters.

3. Pressing Beyond the Dilemma: Elements of Rebirth

The major dilemma of mainline churches today is rooted in the fluid, evershifting environment of modern society. This is a serious problem, but I believe there is a remedy. Perhaps more accurately, the remedy could be described as a set of related elements or factors that, when taken together, enable a congregation to press through the dilemma, surviving on the one hand, and helping people live less fearful, more abundant lives on the other.

I have three specific factors in mind. They are usually present in a congregation through conscious intent, as a matter of leadership policy, not by accident. In broad terms, their power to give life flows from the fact that they provide individuals with a basis for grappling with fear and finding hope. What makes them atypical of churches in general is that they tend to stimulate rather than suppress a candid exploration of relationships and events that occur within a congregation and between the congregation and the world at large. Twenty years from now, we may regard these elements as period pieces, quaintly out of date. For the time being, I believe they are sources of rebirth in local churches.

The first element is **an explicit commitment to assist persons in developing a faith that gives practical meaning to living.** Churches committed in this manner recognize that there is no longer a common worldview, and that the ancient symbols of the Christian faith cannot be counted on to arouse our emotions and guide our wills. As Aelred Graham bluntly puts it, "the days of the doctrinal handout are over." [1] Therefore, these churches try, by methods that stress group experience, to reach the individual at points where he or she seeks a deepened quality to life. This means that the teaching of religion takes its starting point within the day-to-day circumstances of human living. Here, where the dilemma of work, family and society are felt most keenly, fundamental questions about oneself, others, God, and reality come alive. And it is as these dilemmas are sharpened and brought into focus that the search for meaning can best be shared and carried on.

An excellent example of this experience is found at St. Mark's Church, Capitol Hill, in Washington, D.C. Twice a year at St. Mark's, the clergy and trained lay leaders guide groups of thirty to forty persons through an extended period of self-exploration. An excerpt from the pastor's letter of invitation suggests something of the process itself.

If you have been around St. Mark's for a while, you have probably heard that Confirmation Class is a fantastic experience which will change your whole life. In all honesty, I must confess that the life-changing powers of the class are somewhat exaggerated.

Actually, our intention is not to change anybody. What we attempt to do on fourteen Monday nights and two weekend conferences is to give each person an opportunity to be clear about what pressures from within himself (such as fears, desires and values) determine his decisions. It is possible that when a person discovers the basis for his decision making, he may want to change. Or he may be quite content to have his present way of operation clarified and reinforced.

People taking the class are under no obligation to make commitments to the church at the conclusion. They will have the opportunity, however, to see how the Christian symbols and church lore might reflect and interpret the process they have been experiencing. [2]

Some words of Jesus in the Fourth Gospel effectively illustrate the aim of this class: "I say to you, unless one is born anew he cannot see the kingdom of God." What is intended by the leaders of St. Mark's is that the individual discover a new self-awareness, with all that this implies in terms of increased understanding of personal worth, self-contradiction and self-deception, and responsibility for the quality of relationships with others. Their concern is for the exploration of inner space, but in relationship to others and to the basic contexts of community, work and family, as well as to explore questions about the way life is lived and to re-approach religious experience with fresh eyes. As James R. Adams, the rector, indicates, the aim is not to change people, but rather to invite them into a setting in which inner transformation can occur.

What matters most in churches like St. Mark's is not

similarity of educational method. There is enormous variation in method from church to church. What matters most is the conviction that the medium of religion in our day is the common struggle to make sense out of the demands and complexities existence thrusts upon us. It is probably fair to say that here the nature of people's doctrinal beliefs is less important than the practical values by which they live, regard themselves, decide their relationships and interpret the meaning of their place in the world at large.

Why, then, is this commitment to practical meaning life-giving? First of all, because it takes seriously the dilemmas with which we live today. Like all religion, it is concerned with creating the basis for a fully integrated human life. It rests on the assumption that to take responsibility for who we are and what we do with ourselves, we must cultivate awareness of the actual pressures which influence decisions and relationships. Without awareness of our fears and hungers, without a basis for interpreting their meaning in the context of the whole of life, we remain captive to their power and growth in personal freedom eludes us. Faith cannot float above life as a future hope or the memory of a past deliverance and still be credible and nourishing. It must connect directly with the present.

This element also gives life because it produces intense experiences of belonging. Groups such as the ones described by Jim Adams break down human isolation. They permit people to explore the meaning of tenderness and effective caring. They make possible a kind of caring we used to associate with extended families. And, at their best, they help individuals come to grips with the ultimate nature of loneliness — that each of us must reckon with the fact that we are alone and thus, perhaps in spite of ourselves, we come to have less exaggerated expectations of the power of others to make us happy. In the end, by expecting less from others, from our institutions, from our political leaders, from religion's external supports, we are less self-deceived and perhaps inclined to be more generous.

Adams' own words suggest another life-giving aspect. "Those taking the classes are under no obligation to make commitments to the church at the conclusion." Here is a particularly welcome lightness, a relaxation about the institution, its ideology and structure, its need merely to survive. It is as though the church said through its official representative: "We invite you to join us in a journey. Bring who you are, learn what you need to learn that deepens your relationship with people, embrace the unexpected, and be open to new sights that may bring you to a place that we do not attempt to specify."

Eternal questions pose themselves differently to us in different generations. What I like about Adams' words is that they refuse to subordinate the delicate individual chemistry of a person's search for truth to the religious institution's need for uniformity of belief. Christianity through its history has known that union with God is not by way of doctrine, priesthood, right belief or visions of the mind, but rather it is "an experience of realization involving the whole personality." [3]

The second life-giving element I want to mention goes hand in hand with the first. In fact, the second is necessary if the first is ever to flower. **A lot of attention must be paid to the process of inclusion,** helping new persons or fringe members find a trusted place in the church's communal life. The problem facing mainline congregations is not just that of becoming life-examining communities; they must become caring communities as well. Without commitment to self-exploration, caring can degenerate into mere congeniality and self-deception. Without caring, self-search and self-examination are stillborn.

Messiah Church, you will recall, based its approach to new people on the assumption that they should fit into a relatively impersonal structure. There were virtually no efforts made at Messiah to encourage deeper personal ties, to share the richness of personal biographies, to discover people's expectations of Messiah, just as there was no effort made to communicate Messiah's purposes and values. The psychological contract of membership - what people got and what they gave in return for belonging - went unexamined and the barrenness of Messiah's communal life went unchallenged. Churches in urban areas, where few natural communities exist and where the turnover of people is high, must plan and work at the process of including new members.

Let me continue with the illustration of St. Mark's Church,* a community capable of grappling with human trouble and extending care to its members. In 1975, St. Mark's pastor, Jim Adams, was seeking better ways to introduce new people to St. Mark's values and style of life. He was aware that nearly everyone had experienced some significant positive or negative encounter with

---

* The Chapel of the Resurrection, in Arlington, Virginia, appears in another context in Chapter 4. Resurrection's highly individualized approach to member inclusion, briefly described there, offers a useful contrast to St. Mark's Church.

institutional religion. Moreover, these experiences often drastically affected people's view of themselves and their expectations of a church. So Adams decided to establish a setting in which new people and the church's leadership could share in some depth their respective attitudes toward Christianity.

Adams began a series of discussions limited in size to sixteen new persons plus himself and other lay leaders. The content of these sessions oscillated between the participants' significant religious experiences, especially their hang-ups about past religious teaching, and expressions of St. Mark's views on fundamental questions about life, death, God, and human dilemmas. Each session was evaluated with special focus on the manner in which people interacted with each other, including the leaders. By the end of six weeks, a small trusting community had formed. In a reliable, supportive manner, twenty or so people had been introduced to one another. Moreover, they had been exposed to the discipline of self-exploration and sharing at a level that cut below the guardedness of much human talk.

I recently asked a participant in one of these introductory classes what value it held for him. "I developed a group of friends," he told me, "people who really know me better than anyone else except one or two others and my family. I had a chance to learn about St. Mark's, why I am attached to it and put off by it at the same time. Also, I found here that you can talk about difficult things in safety."

I was struck by his use of the word **safety**. Safety, he said, meant he could talk about deeper things in his life without fear of being put down or exploited. For him and others the process of inclusion was built around a dependable group who took him and themselves seriously.

Everything we know about people tells us that such a trusting climate is necessary if people are to see purpose in relaxing their defenses, in opening up their lives and concerns to others. St. Mark's assumptions are that the need for community and meaning is basic and that, given a secure atmosphere, people will actively pursue both. The experience of being known is an essential foundation if people are going to invest themselves in one another. It is a necessary prelude to deeper exploration, facing anxieties, re-examining one's system of belief, learning how one affects others, opening the heart to new questions and new truths.

Here I think it is important, however, to sound a note of warning about the extent to which churches can become caring families. In many clergy and church members there is a deep longing for the church to be a community of love, and even to reproduce the closeness and intimacy associated with early childhood. While it is natural to want these experiences, individuals only set themselves up for disappointment if they expect congregations to provide them to any great extent. Churches are no more perfect than the people who make up the congregation. Our capacity to care is always strained and in short supply. What churches **can** do is help us understand our needs in this regard and learn to live with them on more humanly realistic terms. Nevertheless, having said that, I want to emphasize that it should be the aim of every congregation to deepen personal ties, to build trust, and to establish opportunities for people to give and receive care, however imperfect, from one another.

A third element essential to pressing through the dilemma of mainline churches is **prizing the emotional side of parish life**. Put simply, the emotional side of parish life is the intensity and trauma of living together. It is tenderness, closeness, fighting, hurt, talking through, forgiving, deepened understanding - all the emotional raw material that everywhere constitutes the joy and pain of human life. This should be prized because our emotional life is the soil which feeds our relationship to God and to another. And because if we ignore it, we pay a tremendous cost.

Let us examine the cost. Let us reconsider Messiah's tendency to ignore emotions and value only fact and rationality, because this approach brought a finely organized, efficiently-led church to a grinding halt. Emotions, like ideas, are facts. In any situation, what people feel is as important as what they think. Church leaders who value thinking as logical and downgrade emotion as subjective and irrational actually encourage unreal thinking and decision-making. But even more important, if we create churches which disdain the emotional side of living together, we alienate people from their own inner selves and from each other. [4]

This is not to say that religion is simply a matter of feeling. Religion involves our whole selves - intellect, will and emotions - in our efforts to live well and with purpose. Churches that ignore emotions cut people off from reality. Such churches become deadened, dominated by fear of open speech and authentic feeling, and their people feel burdened with a need to "walk on eggs" with each other. Spontaneity and creative imagination are choked off by the suffocating weight of dullness and boredom.

Why do congregations allow this to happen? Again, because of fear. We fear the intensity of our emotions and prefer the security of deadness instead. But, when we ignore our emotions, we destroy life as well. It means we do not share what moves us intensely, and therefore do not nourish one another. When the emotional side of parish life is ignored out of fear of its power, we are not really spared hurt. We are cut off from one another's affection, convictions, passions, and anger and reinforced in our instinctive desire to withdraw from all significant relationships inside and outside the church that demand commitment, energy and risk. Thus, such churches deepen rather than alleviate human isolation and suffering. They weaken, not strengthen, our capacity to live.

I wish I could say that learning to share the basic dilemmas of living together in a congregation can be done without anxiety. It can't be. But the anxiety can be faced and borne productively with the right guidance from clergy and laity.

To illustrate, let me recount an incident in the life of Christ Church, in southeast Washington, D.C. It offers a striking example both of courageous leadership on the part of the laity and the pastor, and the life-giving promise of valuing the emotional side of congregational life.

Christ Church, a largely white congregation, had just completed a first-year shakedown cruise with its new pastor, Lynn McCallum. It had been a time for establishing new directions based on the desire of the congregation for "a deepened spiritual life" and on McCallum's particular interest in new forms of adult education and in shifting the leadership pattern of Christ Church toward greater shared control. There were the predictable tensions, and some knotty problems, particularly around the operation of Congressional Cemetery (owned and operated by Christ Church) and the parish office administration, which was regarded as careless and, at times, unresponsive.

The pastor's contract called for a year-end evaluation. In several meetings with the pastor and board, it was decided that everyone involved in the leadership needed time, not so much to evaluate Lynn, but to talk over how they felt about the parish, and what they wanted from each other during the coming year. There was strong sentiment for productive sharing, and genuine fears that the disgruntled feelings of several vestry members would get out of hand and lead to unproductive battling. In preparation for a day-long meeting, the rector and vestry completed a questionnaire which elicited their appreciations, gripes and wishes about the pastor and the vestry. The group had been through several strenuous battles that had deepened their trust of each other and of the rector's capacity to listen carefully.

The evaluation day itself was a rich and, for me, moving exchange between candid, serious people. One thorny problem arose that had consistently baffled everyone - the operation of the Cemetery. It was an albatross: it lost money, suffered from continuing vandalism and neglect by city officials, plagued Christ Church with debt, mechanical breakdowns, and caretaker absenteeism. The pastor and the best administrative talent in the church had poured hundreds of hours into improving things, but to no avail. The cemetery drained everyone connected with it. Quite literally, it haunted our work together the whole latter part of the afternoon. We seemed to make no progress with it all.

Finally, one of the vestry summoned courage and said to the pastor: "Maybe if you would really let go of the cemetery and trust the lay people in charge, things would improve." Gently but firmly, other members confronted the rector with the reality of the double message he was giving about the cemetery, saying in effect: "You do it," and behaving in reality, "It's mine, stay out."

The rector listened, reflected a moment. Slowly he began to speak. He voiced several fears he had never shared with them. He said he hated the cemetery. It took him from the work he liked best and did best as a pastor. But he wanted assurance that they, the vestry, would **really** assume responsibility. Also, he feared losing their respect. Giving up the cemetery, he feared, meant acknowledging his limits. At a deeper level, it meant risking their disappointment, possible even rejection, because he had become vulnerable, less than Christlike, another frail mortal like themselves.

When he finished speaking, there was a visible and profound shift of mood in the room. It was clear that almost at the moment McCallum found the strength to voice his fears, he was freed from their power to condemn, and thus able to relax his control over a task he hated. The laity, in turn, reacted with understanding. Subsequently, many of them said that one moment had intensified their appreciation of their rector's ministry, and had taught them something about themselves. Far from alienating rector and people from one another, the incident had helped them find each other. In the months to come, the complex problems of the cemetery slowly assumed manageable proportions.

If there is a moral to this story, it is this: valuing the emotional side of life involves facing real fear, but the promise in doing so is the achievement of freedom. This is the message of the Gospel to us. It is a truth basic to our humanity which Jesus, both by his life and words, sought to unveil and incarnate.

The foregoing are not, by any means, the only conditions of grace and vitality in mainline churches today. Regular reclarification of the congregation's mission in the context of its environment is another. Accurate data about the composition of the membership by age and sex is also an indispensable tool for thoughtful parish leaders. So is knowing how to form effective parish work groups - an element my colleague, James Anderson, rightly regards as usually absent in most churches.

There are other factors. To my mind, however, they are all of lesser importance.

On center stage are the three elements I have described. They are not a panacea. Given our culture's rapidly spreading preference for quick, non-painful solutions to problems, these proposals won't be popular - they require too much hard work. What they can do, however, is set a stage. The central task of churches today is no different from that in the past: it is to help us grapple with the anxiety of being alive in the world, and to find power to live more compassionate, abundant lives.

This period in our history is a time of great turbulence; fear of change and its effects threaten to paralyze our spirit. We yearn for stability. A fresh concern for the practical function of faith, attention to building community and prizing the emotional side of parish life - these three elements set a stage for teaching about the nature of authentic stability. They will make it possible for people to face the radical impermanence of all things, to come to terms with the weakness of human institutions and religious forms, and to be open to the truth Jesus continually pointed to, that true stability is in God, and those who receive it into their hearts as a gift of the Spirit have already learned to cease searching for it. It is a gift precisely because it frees us from the feeling of having to control life, from having to live defensively against change, thus generating in us what my former teacher, Charles Penniman, used to call "a friendly mobility within history" - sitting lightly with fads and cultural heroes, entertaining few fixed expectations, wise about one's fears, open to feeling deeply, and therefore capable of love.

4. What is Meaningful Power for a Parish Pastor?

We have been discussing a core dilemma of modern congregations, one that goes right to the root of their mission in our society. Now I want to turn to another factor which weighs heavily on the effectiveness of church leaders, particularly parish pastors. It is the use of power.

Rollo May has noted that power was originally a sociological category used chiefly "to describe the actions of nations and armies" and that in modern times we have sought a deeper understanding of power in personal terms. [1] It is in this more personal and psychological sense that I want to use the concept of power - "the ability to affect, influence and change other persons." [2]

Until a few years ago, to speak of power and the ministry in the same breath was akin to talking about sex at a Victorian dinner table. May has pointed out that by cultural conditioning we have been afraid of power and have tried to hide its overt exercise from ourselves. Among church people, powerlessness became a virtue, innocence a sign of the moral Christian. Against this background, many pastors have sought to wield influence while appearing as neutral and benevolent parties, as **disinterested** in power.

This climate is moderating now. Psychologists and theologians have shown us that, like generosity and affection, power is essential to our humanity; it is a part of the created order of life. So it is in this positive sense that I speak of power; that it flows from recurring experience of self-actualization - learning to influence others and, in our work and family life, knowing our significance for others. So viewed, power and powerlessness are important concepts with which to interpret current dilemmas in ministry.

In my experience, pastors now encounter the problem of power (and powerlessness) in three ways: **institution-**

ally, as they see the Church's peripheral place in society; **personally,** as they attempt to resolve confusion about their own roles in the parish; **operationally,** as they search for new patterns of congregational leadership that share power in authentic ways.

Institutionally, for pastors, the sense of powerlessness is tied closely to the waning of the Church's influence in society. Despite the current revival in church attendance, the religion of mainline churches is not really integrated with the rest of society. Neither Christianity nor the God of the Bible are now organizing centers for most people's world view. So long as significant numbers of people in society at large granted them the power to "speak, initiate . . . to represent the mysteries of the numinous," [3] clergy had a psychological sense of importance that extended beyond the Church. But as the crises in our civilization have grown, the vitality of Christian forms has correspondingly waned.

As this happened, clergy have discovered that something has ended for them, something they took for granted for a long time - their central place in society. The psychological state created by this chain of events is one of increasing non-essentiality. For many clergy it is accompanied by feelings of self-doubt (even self-contempt), depression, inadequacy, and helplessness which may surface as questions about the worth-whileness of the parish ministry or the usefulness of the pastor's work. These feelings are intensified to the extent that pastors find they share society's doubts, and to the extent that the old religious images are dead or only half alive for them.

More frequently, in my experience, pastors find that their religious values vary significantly from those of their congregation. The pastors remain committed to the original values of service to others which brought them into the ministry, while more and more they doubt the traditional forms of parish life and the once-effective tools of the pastor's craft. If they feel powerless to acknowledge these feelings openly to parishioners or peers for fear of criticism, their vitality and confidence disappear even faster.

Conversely, I have the distinct impression that pastors emotionally committed to older patterns of belief may experience non-essentiality quite differently. Such pastors belong, they feel, to an institution whose truth is quite apparent to them but is regarded by others as empty. For them, the feeling of non-essentiality draws force from the realization that they are part of a defensive, embattled minority, that the Church is no longer woven into the marrow of society's life as it has been

for two thousand years, that their work is less valued,
no longer the formative influence in society it once was.

Personally, however, the experience of powerlessness
arises perhaps more acutely for many pastors **inside** the
congregation. Here what pastors face is the disintegration of a commonly-shared, understood, and clear image
of their role and purpose. Beginning with the writings
of Richard Niebuhr and Samuel Blizzard in the mid-1950s,
no other modern aspect of the ministry has received more
documentation than role ambiguity, role confusion, and
role conflict between congregations and pastors. The
difficulty is twofold. In congregation after congregation there is disagreement about what is the essential
work of a minister. But the powerlessness experienced by
pastors and lay leaders is that they cannot decide how
that question is to be resolved. That is the nub of the
matter and it contrasts vividly with the Church of some
years back.

Dr. Charles Price of Virginia Seminary underscored
the difference between the Church now and then, in a
conversation not long ago. "Role conflicts aren't new,"
said Price, "but we react differently to them now.
Seventy-five years ago, the great evangelistic pastors
preached a clear vision of the Church's mission. They
didn't care very much whether people liked them or not,
whether anyone agreed or disagreed. They were totally
absorbed by their message. And you must remember, people
gave them authority and listened. If they disagreed,
that was their problem, not the pastor's. The same was
true of Catholic clergy - they derived their sense of
confidence from the belief that by the sacrament of
ordination they had authority to speak for God's Church
and interpret His will."

That older church culture resolved differences by
assuming the pastors were right, by endowing the office
with an authority to run the church as they saw fit.
This authority was composed of many factors. Seventy-
five years ago, a level of general knowledge greater than
their parishioners was attributed to clergy. Clergy had
moral power to define wrong behavior and in many congregations to label wrong-doers. In my own denomination, at
least, the leadership resources of laity were vastly
underused. Other Protestant denominations organized
along democratic lines, but in reality, their pastors had
enormous extra-legal pragmatic powers and used them. In
our day this authority has eroded tremendously.

Here again social factors have been at work. People
are better educated. Power has been redistributed by
means of fresh social realities: consumers' and citizens'
groups, management and labor, federal and state legis-

lation, technology, the spirit of participating democracy - to name only the more obvious. Also, we are beginning to find that the complexity of administering any organization today, whether we like it or not, demands more imagination, knowledge, and intellect than even the most brilliant leader can give alone.

One effect of these factors inside the churches has been the growing insistence of laity that the pastor's use of power is everybody's business. So that in numerous congregations the really urgent, often unmentioned questions have to do with how control is shared.

But there is another complicating factor here as well. Much of the research on ministry done in the last twenty-five years points to one conclusion: clergy are no longer equipped with the reliable, theoretical models of their craft, that is, those practical tools for preaching, spiritual guidance, congregational leadership, and pastoral care that connect effectively with the realities of parish life in the modern world. It is clearly not only the disintegration of an older tradition about the pastors' role that now disturbs congregations and clergy. It is much more. It is that we are divided and unclear about how to resolve conflicts between clergy and laity. We are divided about the use of power.

The situation is really worse than I have described. Perhaps the most important reality in all this for pastors is that they are largely on their own in seeking out solutions. This is true despite the progress in recent years of clergy associations and the evolution in some denominations of systems of support for pastors. Still for most, what each pastor makes of his or her relationships with a congregation is chiefly a matter of personal resources. Pastors come armed mainly with their own values and skills, their personality and their essentially private vision of the pastor's functions. With these they must relate to the congregation's unique circumstances in such a way as to forge some pattern of effective influence that increases, if only a fraction, the congregation's capacity for acts of compassion, justice, honesty and integrity.

I judge this last dimension of the crisis to be more important than any other for the short-term future - the next ten to twenty years. Non-essentiality, loss of legitimacy, the need for new tools for deciding questions of control and purpose are likely to remain as primary challenges for congregations for a long time to come. They are, so to speak, part of the churches' fifty-year agenda for redefining their structure and mission in a secular, industrialized society. What is of immediate short-range importance is to establish the confidence of

pastors that they are not helpless, that they can develop
the capacity to work out models of leadership that resolve questions of power, despite the fact that so much
of it puts extraordinary demands on their personal resources.

Certainly from what we know of the psychology of
depression, powerlessness feeds on the conviction that
self-assertion in the face of problems is futile. It is
always difficult to face one's own powerlessness and
confusion. That is why so many pastors and congregations
still ignore or avoid the substantial issues of power
that govern relationships in every congregation, why
pastors often sink under the pressure of carrying on
ministries that disappoint none more than themselves, and
why some pastors leave the parish believing they can be
more effective ministers in secular work.

By themselves crises do not justify despair. Despair is to be without resources, without influence, without significant relationships, or the hope of acquiring
them. As I see it, the short-term task for the churches
is the cultivation of those forces within the Church's
life that encourage pastors and lay leaders to explore
and test fresh forms of influence. When pastors can
confront their own powerlessness directly, they will be
able to rediscover power.

New Perceptions of Power

Power is a social process. In its best forms, power
is expressed as people speak and act together in a climate of mutual respect. Nowhere in the life of churches
does the social character of power stand out so baldly as
when a congregation seeks a new pastor. Here the most
anxious and heartfelt concerns about a prospective pastor
have to do with power: will he or she keep the reins in
his or her hands, use others' ideas or depend on his or
her own? How will differences be handled, things
changed? Is the pastor "mature"? These urgent questions
are a mixture of yearning to be dependent and a desire
for partnership. And they carry the unspoken fear of the
isolation and disregard that results from one-person
rule.

As traditional models of authority have weakened, we
have begun to discover **the meaning of collaboration -**
shared power between pastor and people, church executives
and clergy, in the development of the local church's
ministry. From this perspective, the pastor is seen, not
as **the** sacramental person, but as one sacramental presence among many in a rich, differentiated expression of
functions, talents, individuals and tasks in the congregation's life. Pastors are learning to see that having

influence does not mean calling all the shots.

The new shift to collaboration is paralleled in the Roman Church by the growing importance of parish councils and by the democratic instincts of many young pastors. In mainline Protestantism it crosses denominational lines in both the United States and Europe. It is, for example, notably evident in the attention now being given to systematic forms of clergy evaluation in Protestant denominations such as the United Presbyterian Church, the Church of the Brethren, and the Episcopal Church. To push for new interactive forms of partnership between pastors and laity signals a trend toward understanding the Church's ministry, not as the ministry of one person, but of a community - a communal process in which domination of one by the other is explicitly rejected.

Let me illustrate the principle involved by sharing an incident in my own family. Several years ago, my sons went on a field trip to the National Arboretum. Late in the afternoon they returned home lugging some glass jars in which swam a dozen or so fish they had scooped from a small stream in the Arboretum. These fish were not lovely, shimmering, tropical specimens. They were alley fish - tough, low-slung, brown-water mutts impervious to the tainted waters of the city. We put them in a tank along with plant life, stones, snails, and a water-bubbler.

After a few days the fish began, one after another, to develop a wicked looking fungus-like deposit. Since the infections were spreading, my sons put each newly contaminated fish into a second container. Then we began to notice an interesting thing - while the fish in the original tank continued to acquire coats of fungus, the sequestered fish were getting well. Out of curiosity, we shifted the well fish back into the first tank. Result: fresh outbursts of fungus. Seeing this, we all agreed the fish weren't the problem. The problem lay somewhere in the interaction between the fish and the tank.

The point of this story is one basic to ecological sciences and systems theory: we are shaped by our interactions with the settings in which we live - psychological, social, physical, and organizational. My sons saw that it made little sense to look at the fish by themselves as separate from the tank, as "closed systems" apart from their immediate environment. To help the fish, we had to focus on the ecology of the tank.

One congregation which consciously operates out of an ecological perspective is the Chapel of the Resurrection in Alexandria, Virginia. The pastor, James Green, a friend and colleague of mine, outlined some of the assumptions basic to this view in remarks made not long ago to a group of young pastors in the Episcopal Diocese of Washington:

Our primary aim is to see a caring human community actually develop at Resurrection. So, our policies and behavior as a congregation reflect some of our premises about human needs . . . like a need for belonging. That is - to be related to some people to whom you matter more than superficially and with whom you can let your wants show. Or, a need for self-esteem. To find your talents put to use, to exert your influence in ways that are visible and matter.

We pay a lot of attention to organizational processes that allow these needs to be met. For example, we are in a high turnover situation, so we concentrate hard on the inclusion process. The members and I do a lot of eating together. We have a pretty well thought-out process for helping people move from outside in - we listen for what level people are at, the degree and kind of need they have for belonging and self actualization. Some want to pursue their own personal growth - do their own thing. Others want to work on parish and community tasks in groups or committees. Others like the formal and structured aspects of the church's life and could [not] care less about self-development, community issues or task forces. We assist people to get plugged in at their own level.

. . . . Our theology is taken from Paul's understanding of the Body. The gifts, the resources, are there in any group of people. We try to create an organizational system which evokes them. The metaphor I like is "growing mushrooms." Mushrooms are fast growing and short lived. We encourage people to develop their own standing committees - finance is the only on-going mushroom. We have as little management super-structure as possible. Groups work, don't report; the Vestry gives positive support. We try for a climate in which mushrooms can grow - short-term functional groups who make their own decisions and do the jobs. Long-range planning does not fit our style. I try to help us watch what we do and learn from it. My task as Rector is to concentrate on the stability of the parish and help us be able to change. My basic jobs are to stimulate others, enable them, and coordinate things.

What attracts ministers to a wholistic view of their congregations? It is the lure of order and coherence, the prospect of getting the mind wrapped around an unwieldy complex mess. We know from the study of social systems that action taken in one part of a congregation has an impact on every other part. An "ecological" view gives the designated leadership a frame of reference to appreciate these inter-relationships and to interpret their impact upon the overall climate and direction of the congregation.

Let me sharpen this point with a specific example. Suppose a church's leadership notices that several new families, who have attended regularly for a time, stop coming to church. How might they respond? At least four different levels of response are available: [4]

1. With concern for these families only: visit and talk to them.
2. With concern for events: has this happened before? What were the circumstances?
3. With concern for the whole area of newcomers (a subsystem): is our new family-reporting setup working? Is the calling system adequate? Do we have an effective way to learn from newcomers what they expect and need, as well as communicating our own?
4. With concern for the parish in its entirety (the total system): is there a sound relationship between our purposes, the life needs of people in this community and what we offer? Are there related problems, e.g., a weak Sunday School, a poor quality of worship? What can other new members tell us? Can other inter-related areas like recruiting for tasks, programming, communications shed light on a good process of inclusion?

Feelings of powerlessness among many pastors nowadays have their immediate roots in organizational problems that seem overwhelming and unmanageable. Among the most intractable of these are vague congregational aims, conflicting member differences, fear or ignorance of personal and social issues, a lack of motivation among members, the inability to close gaps between how things are and they way they should be.

The promise of an ecological view is that it supplies leverage for cutting through such organizational and human thickets: a) it can stimulate a concrete formulation of the congregation's purposes; b) it can disclose the church's strengths and limitations in relation to its purpose; c) it can release in a burst of energy, talents and commitment for tasks; d) it can stimulate a spirit of constructive problem solving. In short, an ecological view balances the "cure" of souls with the "cure" of the community itself to which they belong.

These two perceptions of power (collaboration, an ecological view) carry us naturally to a third - a new understanding of the pastor's chief functions. Jim Green's words ably summarize this image: "My task as Rector is to concentrate on the stability of the church and help us be able to change. My basic jobs are to stimulate others, enable them, and coordinate things."

Within my work, I find there are a steadily expanding number of younger pastors who see their central work as a **ministry of leadership to the congregation as a whole,** as distinguished from a ministry to individuals. Leadership of this sort is concretely expressed through certain quite specific behaviors:

a) encouraging the lay leadership to examine the effects of their own policies and actions and to learn from what they find;

b) assisting the members to define their purposes (understood as goals, or general directions) in relation to articulated personal and community needs;

c) prodding the members into active awareness of the impediments between "where we are" and "where we want to be," directing energy toward problem solving, not program production;

d) insuring the open flow of information between parish groups and commissions;

e) consciously attending to the quality of congregational life so that, over a period of time, caring relationships evolve among the members and toward the world around;

f) linking with other organizations and churches in the community and eliciting joint commitments to action on important matters;

g) seeing that policies and plans are tested against criteria of that congregation's values and express the demands of its environment.

Describing the pastor's work in these terms frequently arouses anxiety among clergy and lay people alike because it appears to strip the clergy of spiritual depth. But, in actuality, none of the congregations where this new image now prevails regards the pastor merely as an administrator or a secularized copy of the bureaucratic manager. The reasons why are important. Without exception in these churches, the pastor carries on the ancient functions of leadership in Christian communities:

- presiding over worship, baptizing, and celebrating the Eucharist;

- preaching the Gospel to the gathered community and interpreting prophetically the "signs of the times."

The foregoing discussion of the pastor's work as

cultivating and coordinating the ministry of the congregation to itself and to the world outside closely parallels Hans Kung's description of four decisive New Testament criteria for the service of leadership in the Christian community: 1) the pastor's leadership is a service to the community; 2) it is faithful to the norm laid down by Jesus, which will not tolerate any dominative relationship; 3) it is indebted to the primitive witness of the apostles; 4) it is operative within a multiplicity of functions and services. [5]

Does this perspective help pastors grapple with the nature of their own power? I believe so. First, from my observations of the pastors I know, it carries them toward a coherent and integrated view of their role in the church.

Second, it is open to vigorous, imaginative, theological reflection. In fact, theological corroboration of what many pastors are discovering in practice is found in the works of such different writers as Harvey Cox and Hans Kung.

Third, the new image is capable of professionalization (learning a body of knowledge and skills adapted from specific fields such as social psychology, anthropology, human personality development, and organizational psychology).

Fourth, out of this perspective pastors may begin to learn the difficult art of an authentic resolution of the issues of power within the congregation.

The Necessity of Tension

These perceptions of power - in fact, the entire question of power in the Church - lead us to a basic matter which we often overlook. As I have said earlier, a community of Christians is meant to be life-enhancing - for its members and for the public world in which it exists.

The issue here is whether there is sufficient tension within a congregation to sustain its life-enhancing purposes.

Tension is not a negative state; it is the positive precondition of renewal and rebirth in all organized forms of life. It describes the interaction between people as they search for and carry on the meaning of their life together. In parishes, creative tension arises in those moments when the pastor and members examine and debate seriously the purposes of their life together - specifically, as they deliberately look at different aspects of their life from the standpoint of what actually goes on. This "looking" focuses both on life **inside** and upon the demands the church experiences from **outside,** from the surrounding community. Its purpose is to regenerate a fresh sense of the Church's servanthood and mission out of the perceived gap between where we actually are and where we want to be. Here tension takes the form of stress experienced emotionally as anxiety and the joy of discovery. Unless the congregation has learned to bear the presence of anxiety, it is apt to resist this kind of tension and the activities which produce it. And, of course, the greater the fear, the less tension and the greater the communal stagnation that results.

To demonstrate just how critical creative tension is, here are three brief but important congregational examples.

Consider worship. My own denomination has been engaged in persistent, often anguished search for new forms of worship. This search is often reduced to the level of aesthetic squabbling over niceties of language and patterns of rite. The trouble lies deeper. Our search arose because the symbols and forms of the 1928 Prayer Book no longer interpreted the anxieties and spiritual hunger of more and more people. The very language and rituals themselves became barriers to the experiences of transcendence and integration that they were intended to make possible.

The problem here is more than language, more than a conflict of differing aesthetic preferences, more than the legitimate demands for tasteful liturgical experimentation - though these are all there in the picture. The problem arises because authentic worship is meant to loosen our hold on the illusion that we are in control of life; it is meant to break through our normal ways of looking at ourselves in the world; it is meant to move or shock us into an awareness of our vulnerability.

So by its very nature, worship involves anxiety. And resistance to changes in worship may often be, although this is not always true, an effort to save dead ritual forms which protect us from the anxiety that genuine worship arouses. The more seriously a local church takes the purposes of Christian worship, the more it will experience stress as the precondition of rebirth, new birth.

In a similar way, creative stress accompanies the search for social justice. Suppose a congregation consciously encourages in its members a concerned involvement with community issues. Of necessity, the members will confront conflicting power interests, disagreements with other members, hard choices between policies, opposing theological views on public issues, and personal criticism. Obviously, such a commitment carries a degree

54

of fear and plain discomfort. But unless the necessity of stress is understood, the parish's ability to influence the outside world responsibility will dry up from fear.

What I am saying is also true of church community life. The Christian definition of community goes beyond sociability. It rests upon the assumption that love and freedom flow from sharing and facing the basic problem of living with one another. Here again, unless a parish deliberately and effectively encourages such opportunities, feelings of belonging, acts of compassion, greater personal reality between individuals - all will be empty hopes.

I hope I have made two related points clearly. First, that creative tension is essential to the life-giving process of parish life. Second, unless the core leadership of a congregation knows and accepts this fact, the fear of stress itself will prevent the sustained experience of tension necessary for parish renewal.

This need for tension - both for a congregation's adaptation to change and the realization of its purposes as a community of Christians - creates the most critical power issue of all for pastors. It is their basic task to see that a creative level of tension is sustained. There must be sufficient anxiety for worship, spiritual growth, evangelism, and new learning to occur, but the anxiety must be contained within bounds. It must energize, not paralyze, the congregation's life. And pastors must do this without alienating themselves from the core leadership of their congregations.

The Person of the Pastor

None of this is simple. It is one thing to say that the maintenance of tension, collaboration, an ecological view and a ministry of leadership to the whole congregation are, when taken together, vigorous antidotes to problems of power in parishes. It is quite another to imagine their widespread adoption by pastors and lay leaders, even those intrigued and excited by them. In churches where they have not been the norm, the implied changes accompanying these forms of power predictably arouse stiff congregational resistance. It is difficult to overstate the importance of this resistance both for the congregation's ability to adapt and the pastor's capacity to lead.

Here, briefly, are some of the important sources of a parish's resistance to examining and revising its customary approach to authority and control:
  - a widespread and deeply felt wish to enshrine pastors as heroes. Pastors often share this wish as

well. It is rooted in our fear of creatureliness, of vulnerability. The effect of this wish is to force clergy to be unreal with themselves and their parishes. It makes it tough for ministers to express their own needs, expose vulnerability, be reasonably spontaneous about their feelings, moods, and judgments. The pastor often ends up acting a role.
- high degree of dependency upon the pastor's leadership (one vestige of the older pattern of power) creates a "let the pastor do it" style that is itself a defense against the anxiety of growth in accountability to one another, and of the intensity of real relationships between equals.
- strong needs for inclusion and low tolerance to stress block the development of motivation for congregational self-examination.
- the highly competitive nature of the local congregation's position in the "market" increases concern for stability and squashes a capacity for risk-taking in response to human issues and needs.
- genuine fears of intimacy and self-awareness interfere with the building of community.

These factors highlight the extent to which irrational forces can dominate personal interactions between pastors and members, affecting leadership, parish climate, and programs. Certainly, the single most important figure in this complex maze is the pastor. Perhaps this seems an unfair weight to put on one person's shoulders, but I know of no instance in which such forces have been altered against the will or without the commitment and help of the pastor. Even a body of determined, capable laity is incapable of change with a balky, resistant pastor on the scene.

Where there is no concern by the pastor to soften these factors, no ability for dialogue and shared influences, no pressure for creative change and no will to lead, the church's climate will remain or rapidly become flaccid. Thus, the evolution of new patterns of church adaptation requires the active infusion of the pastors' leadership and a continuing willingness on their part to assume risk.

The Pastor's Autonomy

In many ways, this is the most important point of all I have to make in this book. What our situation requires is pastors with the capacity for autonomy. Autonomy is an extremely over-used word today, with many definitions. Yet it says better than any other word what I want to stress about the nature of authentic ministry.

56

So I want to take some pains to explain it carefully. [6]

Autonomy has to do with people's inner ability to govern themselves. The concept of autonomy, as I see it, does not mean noisy self-assertion, adolescent rebellion against authority, or rugged lonerism.

The autonomy of pastors, for me, is a capacity to balance and resolve opposing demands within themselves and between them and their congregations. It is the ability to do so in keeping with their personal values and intelligent self-interest and with the interests of the congregations in which they work. [7] To borrow a phrase from Rollo May, such a capacity does not imply power **over** the members but power **with** them. It does not contradict the concept of ministry as servanthood, but is its essential accompaniment. In order to sustain a creative degree of tension, to take risks, to be out front about their hopes and intentions, to tolerate ambiguity, to stand criticism, to challenge prevailing norms, pastors must have within themselves the ability to be autonomous persons.

The central criticism usually lodged against Christians who seek autonomy, as I have defined it, is that in doing so they deny the sovereignty of God. I suspect this is to confuse dependency with personal accountability. [8] For Christians, obedience to God does not mean the surrender of self-hood, but a willing commitment of energy, talent, and reason to the purposes of Christ. Refusal to value one's self, on whatever grounds, is false virtue, and may in fact arise out of anxiety as a trick we play in order to force ourselves to abandon the quest for wholeness. In Jesus' parable of the talents, the poor servant is the one who fails to take initiative, to assert his own judgment, and to use what had been given him to advantage.

What does it mean for a pastor to pursue autonomy in an essentially voluntary organization like the Church? That is the question to which we now turn.

5. Pastor and Congregation: a Fragile Arrangement

I have tried to show that parishes capable of helping people grapple with fear must learn to sustain a
creative amount of stress. First, pastors must make sure
that stress is bearable and focused so as to nourish the
search for meaning. (Put negatively, they must make sure
tension and anxiety are not blocked out of the parish's
life together, but channeled so the parish can do its
job). Second, only pastors of considerable personal
autonomy can work effectively with laity to do that.

Now, I want to make some further comments about
autonomy and then discuss in concrete terms its importance for the truly delicate relationships between pastor
and congregation.

Since I believe personal autonomy is essential to
the well-being of every person, I would say, without
qualms, it is the business of pastors to develop a high
degree of autonomy within themselves. Why? Well, let us
look closely at what happens when pastors fail to develop
autonomy sufficient for parish leadership.

A while back a good friend of mine, Dr. John Fletcher, wrote an intriguing paper entitled "Religious Authenticity in the Clergy." Dr. Fletcher, then President of
Intermet Seminary, together with his staff, interviewed
twenty congregations to talk with laity about the most
significant problems they had experienced with clergy and
rabbis. The similarity of response from all twenty was
so striking that the Intermet staff decided they had
uncovered, not a problem, but a condition which they
called "religious inauthenticity" – the inability of
pastors to be real persons with the laity. The laity
describe their discontent in these ways:

> He speaks down to us . . . did not have head
> and heart together . . . pious . . . hypocritical .
> . . lost on a mountain top . . . did not live Gospel
> in his own life . . . treated congregation like
> children . . . could not relate religion and life's

problems. [1]

Fletcher noted there was agreement on other problems - organizational effectiveness, family, and financial difficulties - but the keystone to everything was the pastor's authenticity as a person.

Perhaps some of my readers are already protesting to themselves, saying something like, "How much personal authenticity existed in these laity? Did they candidly confront their clergy or did they passively ignore behavior they didn't like and turn sour with resentment? After all, it takes two to tango." Let me grant the merit in these questions and return to them at a later point. For the moment, I want to accept the laity's plaint on their terms. What stands out about the pastors and rabbis they describe? Aloofness, distance, a failure to ring true? Yes, but I think these are symptoms. There is something else even more basic. The laity in Fletcher's report described clergy who are self-enclosed, preoccupied with their own personal agendas. It is as though they are separated from their congregations by panes of thick glass.

John McMurray observes in this connection:

People become unreal when their thoughts and feelings are at variance, so they are out of tune with their inner life, and that happens because they are turned in on themselves and shut off from immediate and direct contact with the world outside. **Losing the outside world, they lose themselves.** (Emphasis mine.) Their inner life dies and goes into dissolution, and they become ghosts and echoes, the slaves of orthodoxy and tradition. [2]

Such people remind us of the 'hollow men' T. S. Eliot wrote about. They may also remind us of ourselves since all of us have to struggle in some degree with the differences between what we feel and think, what we feel and do, and between ourselves and the world of people in which we live and act. And while we can have sympathy with both the pastors and the laity in Fletcher's study, probably most of us would agree with his diagnosis of them as 'religiously inauthentic.' In my judgement, religious inauthenticity is a by-product of undeveloped, or diminished, personal autonomy. It is the root cause of experiences of powerlessness for parish pastors.

When pastors become self-enclosed - silent about their own personal battles in life, unable to ask for help from the laity, consumed by work, preoccupied with their own religious values, closed against conflicting expectations of the laity, constrained by fear of criticism - they cannot establish the relationships of mutual accessibility and candor necessary for the tasks of parish life. They lose, after a time, credibility with the laity as guides in the search for meaning. Only pastors who struggle to become more free as persons in the company of others are free in themselves to assist others search for freedom. Put simply, that means to work at being continuously vulnerable to oneself and to others, and in spite of painful defeats, not to shut down, but to persist.

In our day it is popular to define autonomy as freedom to do your own thing, free of the claims of others, usually others like bosses, parents, organizations, neighbors who we fear will take control over us, if they haven't already, and block our way to self-fulfillment. That view of autonomy distorts its essential meaning in the service of a type of spiritual isolation that, if successful, completely demoralizes a person's capacity to be autonomous.

The root meaning of autonomy is to be self-governing. To be autonomous is to stand on one's own feet in authentic relationship with other persons.

Now, transpose these understandings of autonomy into parish life. It is apparent that a closed-off, or fearful, or preoccupied pastor cannot build relationships necessary for a church to be self-examining, searching, risk-taking in its life.

People who are capable of introducing or sustaining the anxiety necessary for spiritual growth must be self-governing. They cannot expect to be loved. They need to be able to stand alone, to help others see the illusion behind their wishes for a safe world, to get temporarily on bad terms with others when it is necessary. They need spiritual values founded in the knowledge of human fallibility and aloneness, in the persistent power of human fear to shut down life, in the necessity of facing anxiety if one is to have life and in the conviction that spiritual rebirth is a continuing struggle each of us must ultimately carry on for ourselves in the company of others.

I believe congregational life is meant to strengthen these qualities in people. Beyond that, I believe, it is important to have congregations whose pastors believe it is their business to grow these qualities in themselves. Fletcher's findings about personal autonomy did not surprise me. It is only rarely that one sees congregations which express 'religiously authentic' relationships between the members and the pastor. Occasionally, one finds churches that consistently exhibit human life as it was created to be: reasonably free of fear, spontaneously expressive, sharing pain and hope, celebrative, realistic about the world, turned inward and outward. Such par-

60

ishes are in the minority.

Normal parish life, like normal human life, is not average. [3] It is far more likely to be inhibited by fear, fear of life and the personal intensity of living in depth. And it is in their efforts to defend themselves against the fear of deepening relationships, against life itself, that clergy and laity inevitably render their relationships inauthentic. What we need to remember, and find safest to forget, is that each of us makes choices about how we respond to fear. Moreover, we can change the kind of decisions we are used to making. As Jesus pointed out, we do not have to cheat ourselves of abundant life by perpetually defending ourselves against fear and by isolating ourselves from what we seek.

This freedom is not confined to individuals. It can become an inner condition of parish life. It is my experience that there are powerful forces in congregations which increase the power of fear. Depending on how pastors and lay leaders recognize and respond to these forces, the authenticity of their relationship increases or declines. For the remainder of this chapter, we will examine these factors and discuss their spiritual and psychological impact.

I want to begin by sharing the story of David. It offers an excellent series of concrete glimpses into the pastor's struggle to master fear-producing factors in congregational life.

David was an experienced pastor who had joined an ecumenical group of clergy with whom I worked. This group was composed of eight clergy who met regularly to talk over work concerns and problems. David told his story partly to fill us in on his first year as pastor of St. Helen's and partly to ask help on a particular problem. I chose David's story because he is an unusually articulate, self-perceptive individual, attuned to his own emotions and those of others. Today, some two years later, he is solidly accepted at St. Helen's. But on the morning he presented his story to us he began by saying that the main issue in his new job was that of establishing his authority to lead:

I guess you could say I've been engaged in a popularity contest. I started off at St. Helen's holding myself back, you know, closing up, and it messed me up. St. Helen's was built around nineteen hundred. Our part of the city had a lot of wealth until the mid-1940s. The church was a glittering fashion plate. After the war, the neighborhood changed; black families moved in; whites moved out, and a lot of homes were torn down for apartments.

By 1960, St. Helen's glory was pretty well faded, and we had more property than we could afford to keep.

Before I accepted the call, the council and I discussed the basic problems facing the church pretty well. For example, we have a fairly large endowment from some legacies that brings in about $15,000 each year. We take in about $30,000 from pledges. It's not enough to meet expenses, so a few years ago the council started eating up the endowment to pay operating bills. Another problem is the council itself. Most of them joined St. Helen's in the early '60s well after the church started downhill, attracted by my predecessor's interest in a social-action ministry. They are mostly social-action types, professionals, liberal politically, with graduate degrees and good jobs. Over the past five years, they have put together several good community programs, and raised money from other churches and foundation sources for inner city work. But **they** don't support the church all that well and they don't like to hassle the other members about money. A majority of the members are people with strong ties dating back over twenty, thirty years, government workers with moderate incomes. Neighborhood black people don't come to St. Helen's much. So we were drawing down our principal and doing little to increase our pledge income.

A third issue about which we all agreed is that St. Helen's future requires a strong congregation capable of self support. The obvious people for us to connect with are the middle-class families moving back into the neighborhood. The catch, as I see it, is that these people struggle with things our own council people are scared to look at in themselves: problems in marriage, raising kids, drugs, sex, job success vs. a devotion to family life. We don't have to pull back from community programming to pay attention to these people, but we do have to shift our emphasis and change direction. Playing armchair psychologist, I suspect part of what makes our style attractive to the council members is that social action is a way of not having to look at your own life. My big surprise was that after all our talk the council hasn't really wanted to look at anything; that's been a big disappointment for me.

I had a predecessor whose style was urbane, head-oriented and fast moving. He did a lot of things himself, so the council never had to take much responsibility. When he wanted something, he operated behind the scenes and got it by shrewd dealing. They like being dependent, so it was a good exchange. But one of the reasons they liked me was my openness with them in our talks. They were tired of being rubber stamps, or so they said. They said they felt the congregation really ought to be involved in more of the action.

But after a few months I discovered that knowing about problems and doing something were two different things. Our council secretary came to meetings stoned. Who confronts him? Nobody. It's up to me since I'm the head guy. But that's just symptomatic of their wish to duck unpleasantness. Big questions like where we're headed, money, their leadership roles and mine, who we serve - we shy away from these, nobody seems remotely interested in doing much work on the hard issues.

I tried from the start to win people's support before doing anything, to get them to like me. I figured the best way to do that was not to make anybody nervous until they trusted me. So I sat on a lot of feelings, tried to be understanding and rational about everything. I stuck to bringing issues up for discussion and remaining neutral. I really was pretty scared - it seemed to me I could blow up the whole thing if I was open about my own judgments about what was needed.

It got so that after a while I couldn't stand myself. About six months ago, I began to realize that I hated going to work. I hated getting up. I was tired all the time. It got to the point that I felt like a dead man behind this collar, like I had stopped caring.

Our home life got bad, and my wife really started to complain. Messing up at work was messing up home, too. Finally, she got through to me. She got me to look at how lousy I was feeling. She pushed me to figure out what I wasn't facing. I figured I had a choice - to go on living like a dead man or to start taking risks with my job. It boiled down to which set of bad feelings I was going to live with: self-disgust or being scared.

I began to concentrate at work on what I was feeling and seeing, on what my judgments were; I worked at getting my piece said at moments where I felt it would have the most effect. I began to put pressure on the council. I don't mean I went wild or shouted at people; I started letting them in on where I was, pushing them to talk about the differences between us on key issues. One thing I decided

I had to do was accept the fact they were dependent, and try to move them off that in small steps. I told the council, for example, that I was troubled by our lack of progress; that I knew we had some tough problems to face; that maybe we were feeling a little disappointed in ourselves, and suggested we take some time away to work on them. To my surprise they agreed. I started calling on those new families in the neighborhood, figuring if I can hook them they'll become a new force on their own. I went to the alcoholic secretary and told him my views about his coming to the meetings drunk. He denied it completely. That no longer has me paralyzed, but I don't know where to go next. He still comes to meetings drunk. I need your help on that one. Other than that, the best thing is I'm no longer refusing to be expressive and the place hasn't blown up. It's still discouraging not having more people on my wave length on key issues. When I was Mr. Nice Guy, at least there was the illusion of togetherness. One price of being out in the open is standing on your own more of the time. Things do move, though. Some council members, whom I count on, first felt my pressure would split the council into hostile camps, but that hasn't happened. We are able to say more clearly what we want to each other. I guess I wonder at times if progress will happen fast enough to be worth the sweat. It's still early in the game though.

The major theme throughout this story is David's sense of jeopardy. Fear of being vulnerable to criticism dominated his behavior. One of the first tasks of new pastors is to gain support for their authority to lead. David wisely understood the difference between authority and control, the capacity to have one's advice and insight taken seriously, versus the power to decide what happens. Unlike many pastors, he did not try to establish his authority by controlling parish decisions.

But David did do something else that badly damaged the authenticity of his relationships with the council: he curried favor. To legitimize his authority, he worked at being a 'nice guy,' suppressing his perceptions and judgments about the mission of St. Helen's when he suspected these would produce unpleasantness or tension. He hoped that affability would slowly secure from the council permission for him to be firm, clear, and expressive without risking their rejection of him as leader. I asked David what he felt would be the result of a serious conflict between himself and the council. More than anything he feared his dependency: he was highly vulnerable to becoming isolated. If that happened he felt he would be without influence, neutralized, impotent.

As the months wore on, David suffered the spiritual and psychic consequences of living a lie: he was deadened, depressed, a man for whom life, marriage, and work had lost their savor. David, however, was a lucky man. He possessed self-sensitivity, a reservoir of personal strength and a savvy wife. These three assets combined to awaken him to the potentially lethal results of his failure to face the pain and fear of confronting this council and possibly being confronted in turn.

In David's case, growing self-disgust became the engine of change in him. He could no longer stand the sight of his fear, and the lengths to which it drove him to conceal what he felt and thought. Steadily, although with considerable anxiety, he began to grapple with the problems at hand. It was a triumph of considerable importance for St. Helen's and for David personally when he began, despite his fear of rejection, to share his vision for the parish and his diagnosis of its ills.

Ironically, as David learned later from his council, his currying behavior had several consequences, each of which produced results directly opposed to his intentions. Initially, the council was puzzled by David's efforts to be noncommittal; his cautious behavior contrasted sharply with the spontaneity and imagination he displayed during their interviews before David was called as pastor. As one man put it, "We would talk about an issue, where there was some real difference of opinion, and I suspected David had to have strong feelings, but he wouldn't tip his hand. (To David) I liked your effort to get all sides out on the table, but then you didn't put yourself out. I didn't know whether you had it all figured out and were keeping quiet, or whether you just didn't like to have people argue with you. It left me feeling cautious about how I played my cards."

Another reaction was disappointment from several members who had been influential in hiring David. He had impressed them originally, not only as competent and attractive, but as capable of a more open style of leadership than his predecessor. Said one, "David's fence-sitting, for that's what he did, really surprised me. He seemed tense, passive and distant. You could not get close to him. I could see us lapsing back into our old style of politics by manipulation. I was quite disappointed and found myself pulling back."

David's early strategy to gain power was self-defeating. Designed to win closeness, it created distance; designed to develop his authority to lead, it effectively diminished the personal strength and vision

for the work that he had at his command. By separating
what he felt and thought from what he did, David began to
lose himself and to lose touch with others. He deprived
the council members of the very stuff they needed to
grant him authentic authority: a knowledge of his vision
and a sense of the power and vulnerability of his person.
He became inauthentic because his life energies, shut
down by fear, became disconnected from his actions as a
man and as a pastor.

How much does David's situation and the way he
responded reflect his own personal make-up and conditions
unique to St. Helen's? From the clergy group's empath-
etic reaction to David's story and from my experience
generally, I believe David's is the struggle of numerous
clergy. It is a struggle that reflects the delicate,
precarious nature of congregational leadership more than
the idiosyncracies of a particular parish. What was the
source of David's jeopardy? What makes the arrangement
between a church and the pastor inherently precarious?
Embedded in David's account are three objective facts of
church life today: the voluntary nature of the Church,
the structural dependence of the pastor, and the inescapable presence of the pastor's vision and values. In
combination they form a volatile mix, producing crises
that either deaden human vitality or generate rebirth.

The Voluntary Nature of Congregations

I want for a moment to speak of congregations des-
criptively, in sociological language. Churches are voluntary religious associations. Their stability depends
in equal parts upon consensus about the vision and purposes of the congregation and upon the satisfaction members get from participation.

In this context, consensus does not refer to
decision-making, but to something more organic. Inside a
congregation there exists an intricate network of mean-
ings that supply direction and coherence to the members'
participation. Consensus refers to an agreed-on set of
values, norms, perceptions and behaviors that make up the
portrait of that particular church. For example, during
the first year I was rector of St. John's Church in Oxon
Hill, Maryland, I noticed that on Sundays members of the
congregation enthusiastically carried on whispered conversations over the pews, delighted to catch up with one
another. Inevitably when I entered the church, dressed
in a clerical collar or black cassock, to put sermon
notes in the pulpit or speak to the organist, a stifled
hush settled across the church, people turned and stared
fixedly into their laps or rapidly snatched up prayer
books and began reading. I had not asked them to do

this. In fact, it made me nervous. I liked them better the other way. Their behavior was a tropism, an automatic symbolic response to the presence of the priest. This scene was redolent with messages to me and to them, showing symbolically their traditional agreements about the role of the priest, about their relationship, about the meaning of a 'good' Christian, and about the vision of God that undergirded it all.

This network of beliefs and behaviors is in every church. It varies enormously, but it is maintained by the church's influential members and by the surrounding environment's expectations of a 'good church.' The consensus is like the tip of an iceberg, a small bit visible to the eye while the vast bulk of it lies beneath the surface of consciousness, unspoken and powerful. Whatever form it takes the consensus can be felt as an alive, 'electric' network of symbols and sanctions - it is **there**, a brute, essential organizational fact. Objectively, this prevailing set of agreements gives the church its identity to the world outside. Subjectively, it supports the credibility of important notions about life's meaning and the place its members occupy in the world. These notions continue to feel valid and right because in large measure other members continue to uphold them.

Any threat to the consensus (say women's ordination, moving the altar from its traditional place, or a new Prayer Book) predictably floods the congregation with tension, a mixture of fear and excitement, leading to a crisis.

The arrival of a new pastor is a deluxe crisis. I have observed over a number of years that the way this threat is managed by the pastor and the members during the first eighteen months sets the cement - it determines the degree of vitality or deadness in the church until the pastor leaves.

Unless the disappointments and conflicting expectations which predictably arise between the pastor and members are identified and negotiated by persons who feel equal in power, the process of incorporating a new leader will not complete itself. To achieve inclusion, the pastor must be perceived as one who values the existing consensus, and yet one who has earned the right to test its adequacy and play a part in changing its nature. He or she must be recognized as a trusted person, capable of giving and receiving straight talk.

The early part of this period is widely known as the 'honeymoon' - a time of good feeling, enthusiasm for new beginnings, and a chicken-soup brew of illusions that will inevitably be unfulfilled. The honeymoon itself is a kind of illusion because, like many honeymoons, behind the scenes anxiety constantly lurks. The reason is obvious enough. The person of the new pastor in that setting is largely unknown. John Fletcher describes the slow decay of the 'honeymoon' perfectly:

Everyone smiles and nods at first, but soon the waters of real life start flowing. How are the first conflicts experienced? Typically, the new clergyperson finds that he or she is **compared** to the predecessor, if there is one, and if it is a new congregation, then to various clergy the people have known. Or, there are early **power struggles** with leading laity about the clergyperson's right of entry into programs and priorities that he or she had nothing to do with fashioning. The minister or rabbi has a feeling that the congregation is watching closely, observing moods and moves, weighing, 'sizing him up,' **testing** him or her. [4]

People test, Fletcher observes perceptively, to learn if there is sufficient personal reality in the pastor to "lure him into any kind of deeper level of relationship at which the issues of power, authority, purpose, etc., can be negotiated." [5]

The testing process is also to find out whether or not the pastor can be creatively assimilated into the congregation in a way that preserves its stability while simultaneously keeping open the possibilities of new direction, new learning, and deepened spiritual growth. This process entails pain. Because it is the nature of any human group to protect the status quo, there is an unspoken general wish to avoid confronting the trouble people feel. In fact, the failure to deal at all openly with these issues of inclusion and leadership is well nigh universal in parishes.

There are at least four ways pastors may resolve this crisis, and three of them are destructive. First, they may tune out or actively abuse the congregation's system of belief. So doing, they block their assimilation into the church as persons of trust whose authority is increasingly respected. Failing to become apart, they fail to gain power to lead. The core leadership may seek to oust them through open conflict, or may simply relapse into apathy and avoidance. Second, pastors may adopt the parish's value system whole hog and thus abort their capacity to place creative tension into its life. Third, pastors may passively refuse to face any of the real issues involved as genuine differences surface between themselves and the laity, effectively abandoning the congregation to a life of discord (as laity compete to fill the vacuum) and spiritual flaccidity.

David, you will remember, came perilously close to the third course. Yet David also illustrates the only way I know to resolve the crisis constructively. The critical issue during the first eighteen months is how the pastor and core leaders manage their fears and disappointments with each other. As David so clearly showed, the positive resolution of the crisis demands an act or series of acts of constructive aggression. Pastors must expose their own pain. They must invite parts of the core leadership into active reflection upon their relationship together. They must make themselves vulnerable to the people's disappointment in them and must be prepared to acknowledge their own disappointment in the people.

Pastors usually cannot rely on the laity to take such initiative, inviting them to join in grappling with the pain of unmet expectations and conflicting values. If that happens, it's so much gravy, a testimony to the reality of the members themselves. But pastors cannot surrender their responsibility to see that the process of reflection begins. Either way, pastors must resist the pressures of apathy and fear, both in themselves and in others, that for the sake of comfort steadily push everyone to falsify the significant differences between the pastor and the core leaders.

Once the ice has been broken, both sides can negotiate only if they feel equal in power. But the first step is to break the ice. Doing that requires a considerable degree of personal autonomy. It means that the pastors expose themselves to the ultimate weapon of a voluntary association - the power to criticize, withdraw, and neutralize the authority of the leader. It is quite possible for pastors to refuse the choice, to run away from the trouble. But once they begin to see the nature of what's involved, it becomes harder and harder. David put it best when he said, "It boiled down to which set of bad feelings I was going to live with: self-disgust or being scared."

The Minister's Structural Dependence

A seldom-mentioned fact of church life is the reality of a special, though often unconscious, pressure upon clergy. Lacking a better term, I will call it **structural dependence**. This means that pastors in mainline denominations derive their basic economic support and their vocational identity from an occupational system. This is the situation of the vast majority of Roman Catholic and Protestant clergy. Structural dependence is, by itself, a neutral fact, but it has important consequences for clergy and lay leaders. Structural dependence creates extreme vulnerability in most pastors and is a cause of primary anxiety in many. Awareness of this anxiety may only be dimly present. Its covert effect upon the pastor's leadership style, however, is definite and decisive.

David was a typical member of the church's occupational system. He graduated from a Protestant Seminary, expecting to be a lifelong minister. He used denominational connections intelligently to get interviewed by St. Helen's, near Baltimore, because he liked the East and was drawn to the denominational executive in that judicatory. David supported his wife and three children from his work as a clergyman; he had no other source of income. In terms of the future, David wanted to remain in the full-time parish ministry. He wanted eventually to work with an experimental congregation, exploring innovative forms of worship, education, and community service. He was acutely aware that in his denomination the good opinion of his peers and judicatory leaders is essential to recommendations for this type of work - or any work, in fact, that fulfilled his capabilities.

It is important to understand that the pastor's experience of judicatory power differs strikingly from one denomination to another. In denominations like the United Church of Christ, power over the minister is primarily congregation-based. The members may withold emotional support, staff assistance, and salary increases from pastors they don't like and they can fire them. They can also produce an embarrassing organizational crisis by withdrawing their money or their membership. As a result, pastors may be forced to leave the church, or their denominational executives may become sufficiently disenchanted with them to lose interest in supporting their future career hopes.

On the other hand, the Roman Catholic Church and the Methodist Church are simon-pure examples of hierarchical power over clergy careers. In these systems, power to determine the priest's placement, advancement, and legitimacy within the Church lies far more with ecclesiastical superiors than with the local church.

In denominations like my own, power is distributed toward the middle of the spectrum, divided more evenly between the congregation, the diocese, and to some degree the minister. The local church cannot refuse to pay a clergyperson, or fire him or her; the Bishop cannot remove a clergyperson he doesn't like unless the local church requests him to do so, (though he is free to refuse any such request) and ministers cannot 'legally' leave unless their resignation is accepted by the local church. This amounts to de facto tenure. However, the parish's power over the individual ministers is still heavy. Members can withold money, withdraw, or freeze out the ministers; the church council can effectively neutralize their leadership and can request their resignation; the Bishop can reward ministers by prestigious committee assignments and, by giving (or refusing to give) recommendations for jobs, decisively influence their future.

Moreover, most denominational executives are inevitably torn between the judicatory's survival needs (funds, healthy churches, good pastors) and the strenuous, complex tasks of working toward a more humane, just society. Both sets of needs are often not synonymous and often in conflict. It is not news, nor very surprising, that a church executive rewards those clergy whom he likes personally, or who fulfill best the values of the institution that executive cherishes most.

Structural dependence creates very real psychic and economic vulnerability for pastors, a condition that involves not only their power to lead but their livelihood, their reputation, their vocational identity, their future career. So that to the degree clergy wish for recognition, respect and advancement from those who have a strong influence in the Church's career system, they put themselves into positions of unequal power. What is even more important, to the degree the occupational system supports and affirms their vocational identity - and that is one of its primary functions - pastors are apt to lose their internal freedom to act as authentic persons within the local church.

Notice two things in this connection. First, all the elements of fear tied to the voluntary nature of the Church are inevitably intensified by the pastors' full-time participation in the Church's occupational system. And secondly, notice what this means for them and the congregations. It means that churches and pastors must learn to abandon the cherished pretence that ministers are not vulnerable to the same pressures that burden other human beings. It means, further, that churches and pastors will, if they are to be adaptive and alive, have to learn to look straight at the tangle of emotions and wishes that engulf their relationships. It means that pastors particularly must develop acute sensitivity to the institutional pressures inside themselves that tend to shut down their courage and independence. And it means, lastly, that pastors and lay leaders will have to learn to accept the work of reflection and assessment, strange and new as it seems, as a regular and expected aspect of their lives together and of their servanthood in Christ.

The Pastors' Vision and Values

There is a third aspect that intensifies the unstable character of the pastors' leadership in the church. It is the ministers' own spiritual vision and professional self-image. Obviously, ministers are not some form of spiritualized electronic tape upon which the congregation programs its own consensus and symbol system. In reality, all new clergypersons are threatening (and exciting) intrusions into the life of a church precisely because they bring their own operative values and vision. We wouldn't want them any other way, not if they are to supply energy and directions and to facilitate the spiritual growth and ministries of others like them. In their fine book, **Ex-Pastors**, Jud and his colleagues describe how this operational view evolves. The pastor, they write:

> . . . has been socialized in seminary into holding a definite set of values. He has been trained to do a job on the basis of these values. His peers in seminary and the faculty have reinforced these values, and his own ideal of himself as a clergyman has been formed. This idea of his professional self, we shall call his professional self-image. For many kinds of work, but especially in the professions, the professional self-image encompasses the other parts of life until they are practically inseparable. [6]

This process does not end with seminary. It is a highly dynamic, personal one in which pastors continue to integrate their experience and professional self-image intensively during the first five years of ministry, and then intermittently thereafter, depending on a series of factors: their personal openness to growth, their management of success and failure, the quality of mentors available, peer support, life stage demands, spouse, the clergy development policies of their judicatory, the impact of social change. This being true, I want to emphasize its importance for the incorporation of a new pastor into the life of a congregation. To incorporate him or her means the effective integration of the pastor's spiritual vision about the church's task. Interestingly, the findings of Jud, et al, as to the dominant reason why the pastors they interviewed had left their churches indicate how essential this is. Jud's group of ex-pastors left primarily because of conflicts with the leadership of their congregations about the nature of the minister's work. [7] Jud and his colleagues go on to say:

> . . . dissatisfaction with the work of the church points to a breakdown in the system. First. .

. . a lack of congruence between the manpower needs
of the system and the training of professionals . .
. . Second, the needs of the local church should be
explicit in order to hire pastors who will find
their professional fulfillment while doing the kind
of work needed by a specific church. [8]
In the past I have agreed on both counts. I still
do to some extent. Yet there is a kind of wistful unreality to these comments that I have often engaged in
myself. I do not believe that either suggestion is
really deliverable, or that if we really had the mech-
anisms to accomplish both we would like the atmosphere of
bureaucratic fine-tuning it would require. No, what
struck me about the pastors and churches in **Ex-Pastors**
was the lack of any commitment to working out significant
differences 'on the job,' the lack of any real grasp of
the fact that this is what human beings in a church have
to do to make a go of it and, therefore, a consequent
lack of investment in facing the pain of building a
community of faith together. There is also something
else. Many of the pastors themselves appeared to be
dealing from non-negotiable positions, with unreasonable
notions which seemed to equate their success with pers-
uading others to view reality as they did. They appeared
to me as walled off from the human fears, wishes, and
biases of the people in their congregations. I felt once
again as though I were watching people trying to talk to
one another through heavy panes of glass.
Let me return to something I said earlier. Working
as a consultant to churches seeking a new pastor - as I
used to do often - I always felt as if I was trying to
stuff a roomful of slippery psychic eels into a bag. I
was forever knee-deep in a writhing mass of emotional
wishes and hopes. For example, there is a strong wish
that the process of incorporation be painless. It never
can be. We know that in our heads. Yet there is invariably resistance to planning how to manage the inevitable
disappointment.
There are also pervasive hopes that the pastor can
be smoothly absorbed into the status quo, quickly robot-
ized by the parish systems of beliefs and norms. Conversely, there are strong desires to be dependent, dominated
by the new pastor's values and vision. Churches do not
hire a pastor, not at first. They hire a knotted tangle
of messianic, erotic, parental wishes and hopes dropped
crazy-quilt fashion on the shoulders of one finite,
limited individual.
Pastors come into this atmosphere, not exactly as
lambs to the abattoir. They carry a heavy bag of their
own illusions, values, and fantasies. They hope against

hope that these will somehow be painlessly fulfilled. But in fact the process by which they gain authority to lead the church is one of substituting fantasy (e.g., that they are invulnerable, omnicompetent) with a measure of reality. It means that the congregations and ministers have to develop the capacity to see and treat each other as real persons, not the projection of unfulfilled wishes. Obviously, this process cannot begin, let alone occur successfully, without reflection, a degree of fear, sleepless nights, and not a few exhausting meetings. It occurs as people learn the ability to say to each other specifically what they appreciate, what they miss in their relationships, and what's important at the heart of their lives.

Here is a short case in point - the problem of time, the pastor's curse.

Some time ago the lay training committee of St. Alban's Church, a training congregation for Intermet Seminary, held its yearly evaluation of the candidate pastor, John Kitagawa. In what was an essentially fine evaluation, one issue surfaced that impressed all of us. John was perceived by the committee as "rushed," "overworking," "spread far too thin" - a pastor who appeared enslaved by work pressures outside his control. The rector, Ted Eastman, acknowledged doubts about his ability to help John since he suffered from the same malady. And then to my surprise and delight, the men and women around the room began to say this was not just a clergy problem, but their problem too. "Maybe we can begin by helping each other," they suggested.

What drives many pastors to have trouble managing their time? As you can guess, my answer is - fear. I have felt it in myself. Keeping busy makes you less vulnerable to criticism in a job that few laity understand, and by keeping busy you show you have something to do; fear of not being needed; fear of the retribution we dream comes like the Furies to all pastors who say, "No;" fear of owning up to your own limits and thus revealing to everyone that you cannot be counted on (unlike your predecessor) to reassure them in their wish to be invulnerable to life.

There is no humanly good way to resolve the presence of fear except by embracing it. No single answer I know exists for the pastors' problem with time except this: they and the laity must grapple with it together, acknowledging motives that in the past good Christians have feared to confess to each other. I would say, categorically, that if, after three years the subject of the pastor's priorities and style of leadership is not a matter of explicit conversation between himself or herself and the laity, fear dominates the scene.

But while fear is inevitable, it need not own us. Ultimately the process of legitimizing a new pastor's authority is one of negotiation in which real people sit down, despite their fears and fantasies, and talk together about real things: the demands of the environment upon the church, who the church will serve, how resources and talents can flourish, who does what, and how they'll know it is getting done.

Out of this process evolves mutual ministry. Also, out of this process evolves an authentic professional image of the pastors, integrated into the church in a way that reflects their actual talents and limits, and builds upon the authority of their internal vision for the church. Failing that, both the church and the pastors will remain enslaved by expectations of mythical proportions that force everyone into unreal roles, and that deaden what might have flourished.

A Fragile Arrangement

The arrangement between a pastor and congregation is fragile indeed. The process of incorporating a pastor into a church is beset by the precarious nature of leadership in a voluntary organization, by the structural dependency of the mainline pastor, and by the driving force of his or her own vision and values. In each case, fear is the most important emotional force. Fear blocks the power of the laity to express themselves to pastors (except perhaps ineffectively or destructively) and it blocks the power of pastors to speak their mind to the laity, caringly and thoughtfully, without jeopardy. Fear-dominated churches push people to become tense, uncommunicative, and unreal with each other.

The solution, of course, lies with each of us, clergy and laity alike. But I am absolutely convinced that pastors cannot rely on the laity to begin the task of calling attention to the trouble between them.

Returning to the question of the laity in Fletcher's study - just how religiously authentic were they? The question is a natural one, but it misleads us into missing the point I have tried to emphasize. It is true that even a highly autonomous pastor has difficulty facing up to core leadership that is impersonal, unauthentic, fearful. This is, however, the pastors' task. It is **their job** to open up these questions, it goes with the territory. As David discovered, the decision to face the fear of rejection and act, despite its power, was the only direction toward freedom and wholeness. I am not saying that pastors are the only source of spiritual power and courage in the church, but as the designated leaders they are the model. In the beginning they must persistently introduce creative tension into the congregation's life or else reaffirm its presence. And they must be prepared to begin alone.

Last month, a pastor of my acquaintance and I were driving down Wisconsin Avenue to a meeting. He is young, one of the ablest clergy I know. I have always been impressed by his manner - a kind of shambling, graceful, lazy relaxation. I asked him about that. His exact words escape me now. They were something like, "Part of it is me. Part of it comes from a decision I made a couple of years ago that I could walk away from it all and still be OK."

Because such a quote out of context is readily misunderstood, let me say he did not mean to imply he wasn't always available, or he did not care, or that he was never afraid. He meant he felt free and therefore could act freely. He had the autonomous power to differentiate himself from the congregation. And so he was free not to be drawn under by its inexhaustible, all-demanding claims.

In today's church, the pastor's ability to lead with authority is, above all, an act of personal autonomy. In particular, it involves a capacity to face fear in oneself, to share influence, to lead the membership into reflections upon the meaning of life together, to build an atmosphere where the irrational forces of church life are taken seriously, to have the courage to reveal one's own needs and judgments and to be accessible to influence in return. To be sure, religious authenticity requires not only autonomous people, but autonomous relationships. Yet pastors cannot wait for someone else to begin; they must have Abraham's vision and courage - to start alone the journey with its unforeseen ending.

6. *Effective Influence and the Fear of Powerlessness*

> Power is actualized only when word
> and deed have not parted company,
> where words are not empty and deeds
> not brutal, where words are not used
> to violate and destroy but to establish
> relations and create new realities.
>
> **On Violence,** by Hannah Arendt

As much as anything else today, pastors are confronted by the question, "What is authentic congregational leadership?" What does it require in terms of knowledge, skills and personal maturity?

Two things are certain. First, pastors are highly vulnerable to organizational and social factors that tend to undercut personal initiative, wise judgment, and courage. Second, an adequate view of the pastor's leadership role must take seriously the impact of anxiety upon his or her capacity to lead. In previous chapters I have pointed to major factors which threaten the pastor's morale - structural dependency, economic and psychic vulnerability, and the minister's declining social status. Taken together, their impact all too often forms a destructive cycle. Structural dependence and loss of traditional authority combine to build a climate of vulnerability for pastors. Vulnerability produces anxiety. Depending on how they react to anxiety, pastors may lose confidence about their power and influence, and give poor leadership. That in turn deepens their feeling of vulnerability, starting the cycle all over again.

I want to emphasize once more the critical role played by the pastors' own feelings of anxiety. These can be, quite literally, devastating. The following story offers a poignant example.

The minister in this incident was an able, intelligent man in his forties, the senior pastor of a wealthy country church. At the time of this incident he had become embroiled in a hot fight over a series of public meetings, held by the church's social action committee, on school busing. One morning, at the height of the battle, a member of the church telephoned to ask the pastor to visit her husband, hospitalized with severe chest pains the night before. He agreed. The wife was a regular member, often sharply critical of the pastor; her husband rarely came to church. When he entered the hospital room the pastor found the man resting comfortably and eager to talk. Later, as the pastor was preparing to leave, the man asked if he could receive communion. The pastor replied it would only take a moment to go to his car, get the service vessels, and return.

As he left the room, the pastor met the man's wife in the hospital corridor. He stopped and invited her to join the service. She turned upon him, shaking with sudden fury. "You can't do that! Don't you know he's a dry alcoholic? One drink of wine and he'll start all over again. No! Never! I won't have it!" Stunned, the pastor tried to calm her. He explained her fears were groundless. To no avail - she was adamant. At last the pastor acceded. Returning to the husband's room, he told the man he could find no communion bread in the car and would come back the next day. The man nodded and said nothing.

In the morning when the pastor returned, the man greeted him in a cold, level voice, "I overheard your conversation with my wife in the hall. I decided to ask the Catholic chaplain to bring me communion. You have no obligation to me. Please go." The pastor struggled to speak, found no words, and walked slowly from the room. Later on, in answer to a question, the pastor recalled his feelings. "There were things I could have done. But I froze. The busing fight had me gun-shy. When she leaned on me, I could see her stoking up a whole bunch of angry people if I didn't do it her way. I didn't need any more of that, and told myself I could come back and talk it out with the man later. When I found he knew I had lied, I felt stupid and silly. Before I knew it, I had walked out on him a second time."

Any seasoned pastor knows the crippling power of that sort of anxiety. What may not be so clear is that such anxiety, in varying degrees, is an inescapable part of leadership, and that learning to recognize and interpret the meaning of the anxiety is a necessary part of reducing its awesome power.

While we still put the minister at the top of the

organizational chart and underscore his or her authority with ordination rites and ecclesiastical law, the fact is that the influence of pastors is sustained increasingly through another less visible medium - that of their own interpersonal transactions. It is through an elaborate network of human relationships that they actually motivate, direct, challenge, and in short provide leadership. The net result is that as the preeminence of their own personality appears larger, so does their vulnerability to personal rejection.

Thus, it is no accident that "conflict management" has come to be a major theme in clergy continuing education programs. Not only does it reflect social change and the new pluralism in congregations, it expresses the critical importance of conflict for pastors personally. For no matter how well prepared they are, the eruption of conflict, particularly as a result of their own words or deeds, is never routine. All serious conflict threatens to weaken or uncouple altogether that network of reciprocal relationships through which they wield influence, leaving them rejected or isolated, and eventually powerless to lead.

There is a serious problem in this for both pastors and congregations. Few of us relish psychic pain for its own sake. Instinctively we seek out experiences of appreciation, and just as instinctively shun the risk of rejection and criticism. It is predictable that over the course of time the pastors' vulnerability to rejection will blur their capacity to distinguish between what the congregation requires and what influential groups (or powerful individuals) want. So, in the normal course of events, the anxiety of their position makes it increasingly difficult to choose a course of action based on its inherent values for the church in preference to one that minimizes personal risks to their network of relationships. Often the very presence of such feelings goes unnoticed by the pastors or is so thoroughly unacceptable to them that they fail to examine the effect on their behavior.

That is why the question of effective leadership is tied so tightly to the pastors' understanding of these structural dilemmas. In my experience, pastors develop different ways of overcoming the threat of rejection and establishing power for themselves within the congregation. Some ways are clearly more productive forms of leadership than others - for both congregation and pastor. In this chapter, I want to describe four kinds of influence and discuss them, citing their consequences for the local church. [1]

Broadly speaking, the ministers' leadership style

includes values, personal qualities, concepts, rules, strategies, in sum, all those behaviors manifested while they lead the congregation. A strategy of influence is only one aspect, though a decisive one, of pastors' leadership styles. It is the one type of influence they use more than any other. It is their characteristic mode - the way they actually rely upon, especially under stress and with varying degrees of self-awareness, to influence others. Two things should be emphasized about pastors' strategies of influence. First, they represent their personal solution to the problem of power in a voluntary religious community. Second, whatever the type of strategy, it has a vital impact on the congregation's spiritual health and adaptiveness.

The first kind of power outlined in the next section is an example of influence that enhances the pastors' ability to build effective leadership ties and the community's ability to interact in a sensitive way to its environment.

1. Integrative Influence

Hannah Arendt says about power, "While strength is the natural quality of an individual seen in isolation, power springs up between men when they act together and vanishes the moment they disperse." [2] Integrative influence is power in which the key parties are accessible to each other. In congregations, it has the sense of mutual influence between the pastor and laity, an equalization of power in which both mold the other but neither dominates consistently.

A striking example of integrative influence was recently told me by the pastor of a midwestern congregation of some three hundred families. His judicatory executive, upset by conservative outcries against a growing number of local church innovations in worship, sent a chastizing letter to every pastor, asking them to conform to a very restrictive set of judicatory guidelines for worship. This pastor belonged to an innovative liturgical parish. He described his reactions:

> At first I was angry. We were being spanked like eight-year-olds. Then I thought, Wow, I'm in hot water. The conservatives will jump on this letter and use it to force a return to the traditional style. My first impulse was to duck the whole thing, not tell anybody about Tom's (the church executive) letter. Obviously, that wouldn't work. My next idea was to go to the people and say that despite the letter we would continue our present practice. After all, Tom has no legal authority to make us comply. Later that week I had a talk with

Kevin, a colleague, which triggered another thought. He had already told his people they would go along with the letter even though it caused hurt and anger to do so. I felt that was a childish thing to do. Sort of malicious compliance - they go along, say nothing, but end up resenting Tom. Well, it finally occurred to me that this was a great opportunity for us to work out the meaning of worshipping and also talk over how we deal with authority. It invited a head-on clash between different camps. The church council talked over my ideas at length. Eventually, we decided the opportunity was worth the risks involved and that we could handle the problem.

So, early in September, I read the Executive's letter at every service. The question is, I told them, what is our response? As their pastor, I said I had decided with the board that we would work out our answer **together** as a congregation. There were two conditions: there would be no deadline for our decision and we wouldn't back off from the work by taking refuge prematurely in simple defiance of Tom or in going along with him. Next, I introduced the head of the worship committee who spelled out the overall plan and the first activity - a series of Sunday meetings in small groups to talk about our needs in worship, and how our practices help or get in the way. I indicated we would continue our worship as usual and inform Tom of our decision and our intentions. The people responded well. We really have begun to learn a lot about ourselves and some of our problems. It's like a million volts of energy charging around the congregation. Right now we have two people preparing for the next stage - a public debate and more small group discussion on the authority issue.

The point of this example is that integrative influence embraces, instead of avoiding the risks of sharing control. For their part, the pastors take into themselves and live with the tensions between their own personal wishes, those of the congregation, and the demands of the environment. In their interactions, both the pastors and the key lay leaders treat each other as partners, informing (presenting facts, ideas, experiences, judgments) and exploring (eliciting facts, ideas, experiences, judgments, using each other's resources) together until a decision is worked out. [3]

The threats to the pastor and the church in this example were active, palpable dangers:

-    The pastor risked personal criticism and loss of face (e.g. the congregation might have refused to

participate; liberal groups could have perceived his plan as a threat to the new status quo and attacked him).
- He risked losing influence (e.g. a congregational decision that went against his expressed preferences).
- The Board risked a divisive conflict, extra meetings, sleepless nights, fighting, loss of money and members.

Despite these risks, the anxiety in the situation was tolerated, not sidestepped nor avoided, thereby permitting an intelligent appraisal of options.

Significantly, the people experienced the pastor as forthright about his feelings and judgments. Certainly that requires courage and involves a personal response to criticism. But at the same time it builds a climate of trust and of joint partnership in setting parish directions.

The positive consequences of integrative influence for a congregation are potentially high. The development of mutual control by a pastor over the course of time can foster a number of healthy processes:
- the creative tension necessary for spiritual growth;
- energy for tackling problems;
- energy for responding to the community;
- flowering of member resources;
- negotiation of conflicting interests;
- respect for differences;
- tolerance for ambiguity;
- more imaginative leadership;
- greater self-examination;
- exciting accomplishment.

2. Reactive Influence

A second type of influence is reactive influence. Here the pastor attempts to gain power through compliance with congregational values and expectations. In essence, the guiding principle for the pastor's leadership behavior in key situations is to gain and hold member approval and thus retain a degree, albeit a limited degree, of power.

A recent newspaper article illustrates this kind of influence. The story featured an extremely successful suburban church. Every Sunday throngs of people jammed its services. The format was a restyled version of an old-time medicine show - bouncy music, promises of miracles, programmed friendliness, a money-back guarantee to first-time visitors. Explaining his strategy to the reporter, the pastor said few people come to church on

Sunday to hear about problems or to be reminded of pain. They need instead "to be distracted, reassured, and given the feeling of being part of a fun-filled family." By tailoring his leadership behavior to the members' wishes for a problem-free life, this pastor gained a dramatic degree of personal leverage.

The basic aim of reactive influence is to reduce or prevent tension between the pastor and the laity. Thus, it serves as a shield against the anxiety that wells up whenever the tragic divisions of life are taken seriously. Reactive influence serves an important psychological need for pastors. It stabilizes their position within a voluntary community, providing an immediate protection from the anxiety of occupational failure and of personal powerlessness.

What makes this form of influence doubly seductive are its very real positive aspects. Reactive influence gives room for the pastors' nourishing and supportive roles. It permits a steady contribution to the church's stability. And, at its best, when coupled with leadership sensitive to people's need for community and nurture, this form of influence builds firm members' bonds. The basic difficulty is a spiritual and human one: by denying the authentic struggle of people it fails to offer genuine comfort or to provide any prophetic illumination of the social situation in which the church finds itself.

There is also another problem here. Many pastors who respond to the stresses of leadership by reactive strategies become depressed. As a strategy, reactive influence results from strong internal wishes in the pastors to be liked, to be dependable, non-rejecting persons. The resulting accommodation requires that the pastors devaluate the worth of their own judgments, suppress feelings of anger and disappointment, and tune out creative insights that arouse tension in people. All this is usually accompanied, with rare exceptions, by a denial of their own apostolic function, that of confronting the idols of the people or establishing conditions in which those confrontations regularly occur. To deny continually the worth of one's deepest convictions, to allow one's views and behavior to be shaped largely by others, weakens the pastors' energy for work and their self respect. Eventually it leads to chronic feelings of inadequacy and lack of accomplishment. Like the victim in Poe's "The Cask of Amontillado," the pastors become walled-off, separated from the deeper parts of their true selves which, over time, are layered over.

The consequences of this kind of influence for the congregation are mixed, but chiefly negative:

-   loss of tension necessary for spiritual growth;
-   limited ability to respond to the church's social environment;
-   avoidance of important value differences;
-   high sociability, atmosphere of caring, family feeling;
-   high stability;
-   lack of risk-taking leadership;
-   copping out behavior from leadership, including the pastor.

3. Proactive Influence

This is the pastor's assertion of power **over** others. It is unilateral influence by which pastors try to re-shape the basic consensus within the congregation. They decide what is to be done and how. They consciously work to give the appearance of not manipulating, yet at the same time carefully manage the strings of power, as in the advice once given me by an older pastor when I was about to become a rector for the first time:

Remember, you have to keep the power in your hands. Work behind the scenes, not out front. Plant seeds - then people will later think of them as their own ideas. When you want something, line up the most popular man on the vestry and, if you can, the most powerful. Deal one on one, never with the whole group. Help everyone feel important without becoming powerful. Keep your own counsel, and remember, your face can give away your thoughts.

Proactive influence also may be less subtle, employing open coercion or heavy persuasion in a process of direct domination. In effect, the message picked up by the laity is: "You must do what I want because I have the power and knowledge to decide what's best for you."

Proactive strategies thrive in a church climate where the members view themselves as helpless and the pastor's exertion of power relieves them of responsibility and anxiety. Also, the proactive pastor can inject great zest and energy into a congregation and often achieve, by sheer dint of charismatic power, difficult parish objectives.

How does this kind of influence relieve pastors of anxiety? In the first place, proactive influence may in fact involve pastors in the anxious burdens of self-assertion just as fully as integrative influence. Many social-activist pastors of the past decade spoke and acted out their vision of the Church, despite considerable risks to their economic and professional future. Certainly, in its volatile forms, proactive leadership is a direct threat to parish stability and a proactive pastor may face the prospect of rebuilding the congregation if he or she survives. But it is hard to distinguish courageous forms of proactive influence from forms in which the pastor is simply autocratic or pathologically willful. In these latter instances, the pastors simply do not feel anxiety about their position, or use proactive behavior to show themselves that they are masters of their own fears.

Second, as a strategy, proactive influence can protect the pastor from the dangers of taking seriously the opposing or differing needs and opinions of church members. This is true particularly if pastors feel in danger of being sucked into the gravitational field of these members' influence, and losing influence or authority altogether. Fears of powerlessness often flow from the threat of having their influence neutralized, being 'taken over' by a powerful clique or strong aggressive lay leaders.

Third, by skillful manipulation, pastors are rewarded by 'making things happen' and yet escape direct vulnerability since their intentions are seldom clear enough to challenge and their actions remain veiled behind a screen of calculation. Sometimes, pastors will manipulate others unwittingly because their own natural needs for power are unacceptable to them, (e.g., they believe them to be 'un-Christian') and are blind to the controlling impact their behavior has on others.

As a contemporary strategy of effective leadership, proactive influence has a few attractive features and many serious defects:
- high tension, which is at times creative;
- it fosters dependent laity;
- increased emotional distance between pastors and members;
- little negotiation of differences;
- often high administrative competence;
- often weak problem solving;
- mystery about pastor's intentions;
- win-lose fighting;
- game-playing relationships;
- productive program activity.

4. Inactive Influence

Inactive influence is preoccupied with irrelevancies and can become rapidly mixed up in the petty trivia of parish life. It is a kind of non-leadership. The pastors are disengaged from personal and social issues - they simply tune them out. Unlike reactive influence, in which the pastors may focus on certain problems legitimized by the lay leadership, inactive influence remains entirely above serious involvement with important internal questions or community tensions.

An example comes from a story related to me by some old Washington friends, who moved to the midwest several years ago and recently returned for a brief visit. For six months they attended their neighborhood church. Not once during that period, they said, had they heard a sermon which addressed a serious human or social concern. The sermons were, instead, theological discourses, well planned and well delivered, yet abstracted completely from the lives of the men and women sitting in the church.

Perhaps the best illustration for church leaders of inactive leadership is the repetitive tedium of many church board meetings, so stifled by organizational procedure and the details of plant use that the sharp edge of exciting or troubling concerns is continually blunted.

In this form of influence it is especially important to separate style from substance. Inactive influence can be used by pastors whose style is otherwise highly visible. In particular, I think of clear-cut styles in which the pastor's behavior is strongly emotive - evangelistic and emotional, or decorous and immensely charming. Despite the appearance of energy and purpose in these forms, the pastor remains quite detached. As a result, the attention of the congregation fails to focus on important problems, member resources lie dormant, problems are ignored and consciousness of the world around remains cloudy.

Inactive influence resolves the problem of powerlessness for pastors by building a psychological refuge against it. It insulates pastors from the likelihood of confrontation and important risk-taking for the reason that, like reactive influence, it rapidly develops political support. It appeals to ever-present, strong wishes for calm and polite, but unrevealing, relationships. Congregations where this leadership prevails are like those marriages where the spouses never fight - distant and polite, but without zest, spirit or strong affection.

The threat of personal powerlessness to pastors here remains low for another reason. Inactive influence allows them to define success in terms that are non-change-oriented or non-developmental. Thus, the painful possibility of failing to measure up to their own standards of personal effectiveness is enormously lessened. As a method of leadership for congregations, inactive influence is a clear and certain formula for spiritual stagnation.

One cautionary note: my own clear preference for

integrative leadership should not be construed as con-
demning **any** use of proactive, reactive, or inactive behaviors.   In my judgment,   the best leadership behavior
is situationally focused.   The pastors' decisions about
leadership are based as much as possible on their best
assessment of what is called for in particular situations.   They may decide on any occasion to withdraw, or
take over, or to go along.   Such intelligent flexibility
is probably desired by most of us.   Two things distinguish a strategy of influence from any particular leadership act on any particular occasion.   First, its characteristic and consistent use by pastors.   Second, its
importance to them as a way of managing the vulnerability
of their position and of avoiding the loss of personal
power in a voluntary religious community.

Further Examples of Integrative Influence
The more pastors grow as persons, become capable of
autonomy and authentic integrative influence, the more
the congregations can enter into their healing and prophetic tasks and the more fulfillment pastors find.
Likewise, the more the congregations grow in their capacity for creative tension, the more room there is for
pastors to provide them with forceful, clear leadership.
Both conditions require that pastors face into, not evade
or retreat from, the anxiety of their position.   Because
this is such an important element of integrative leadership, I want to cite several additional examples which
illustrate the constructive power that results when a
self-discerning pastor accepts this kind of stress.

Example 1
This incident occurred in a large, middle-income
congregation in a settled residential area.   The pastor,
in his mid-thirties and there three years, regarded himself as a capable organizer, with a talent for adult and
children's education - a high priority in the church.
His predecessor made all major decisions, ran every key
program and left behind a core of devoted, but highly
dependent, lay leaders.   Since coming, the young pastor
had felt a deep-running tide of passivity in the congregation - an inability to generate independent ideas or
follow through on responsibilities, a cloying expectation
that he "will do everything."   Intentionally, from his
first interview for the job, he made clear his conviction
that a parish climate of mutually-shared power and self-
examination was essential if the church were to respond
faithfully to the purposes of a community of Christians.
In May, the education committee, the church's most
able group of leaders, agreed to take from the pastor the

task of organizing the Fall church school program. They carefully laid out the work to be done that summer. The pastor agreed to serve as a resource to the committee and give guidance to the committee chairman at the chairman's request. It was understood the committee would handle all problems as they arose. These arrangements were subsequently communicated by the chairman to the church's membership.

Upon returning from vacation in late August, the pastor found everything in disarray: a third of the teachers were unrecruited, development of the intermediate curriculum had not started, the committee had not met since he left. Almost immediately, the pastor received a telephone call from the chairman. He said he was over his head at work and asked the pastor to recruit the other teachers. The pastor, battling his own feelings of anxiety and anger, reminded the chairman of their agreements with the committee. Reluctantly the chairman agreed to call an immediate meeting of the committee. Meanwhile, the pastor received a flurry of upset phone calls about the fall program. Clearly the basic assumption that only the pastor is accountable was operating at full throttle.

Questions beset him. Had he pushed the committee members too fast? Dare he risk the integrity of the entire program by not stepping in? Should he intervene forcefully and take the reins? If the program limped badly, he would catch a lot of personal hell, look inept and fall short in an important area. If he allowed the committee to shoulder the blame, he would earn their undying resentment. He was sharply aware of his disappointment in the chairman, and the strength of his impulse to bypass him. He decided, finally, that if he allowed his anxiety to push him to freeze out the chairman and to take the pressure of responsibility off the committee's shoulders, no one would take seriously again his publicly-stated intentions to work collaboratively. Moreover, the capacity of everyone to become accountable in each other's eyes would be immeasurably strengthened if he did not absorb all the pressure.

At the special meeting, the pastor made only two contributions. He suggested a procedure for identifying and handling the problems they faced and clarified his expectation that the energy for their solution rested with the committee. Within this structure, the committee and the chairman set to work. Among their decisions were two particularly anxious ones - they decided to delay the opening of the intermediate classes one month, and they agreed that they, not the pastor, should communicate the rationale for their decision to the congregation. Everyone felt considerable satisfaction with the outcome. The pastor's style made a powerful impression on the committee. From his perspective several years later, the pastor designated that meeting and the subsequent events as the turning point when the dependency norm within the church began to shift significantly.

Example 2

This event occurred at St. James Episcopal Church in Wilmington, North Carolina, a county center for professional services. The congregation is well-to-do, with executive and professional families among its members. At the time the pastor was William Dols, who was highly regarded throughout the Episcopal Church in that part of the country.

For several years Bill had been involved in state and national church activities. No one at the church complained openly about the amount of time he spent away. But he was increasingly troubled by his own behavior - he found himself concealing his absences, lying about his reasons for them, working extra days and nights to make up. He became nagged by the fear of being found out and criticized for not doing what the people expected of him.

On a weekend in early Fall, the vestry and Dols spent two days away talking about the congregation's life. Each member was asked to list and share "those things from the previous year which made you glad or sad, about which you want to know how the others felt." On Bill's list were the words, "extra-parochial activities, national Church, community." Bill said he personally was pleased about these parts of his work, but would like to learn how the vestry felt. Later that evening, two members suggested that if he were bothered by these things he should present his misgivings to the vestry and ask for a candid response.

The risks in coming clean were not hard to see. Dols was heavily involved outside. Inevitably important things got overlooked at the church; just as inevitably some people resented his outside involvements. If he came clean to the vestry, in effect he invited their influence over his schedule, declared his investment in them, and implied an openness to compromise. Leveling would make him vulnerable to their criticism and their control. What if they became angry and insisted he restrict himself? What if they turned a deaf ear to his own needs and cut him off? On the other hand, perhaps they might be able to help him organize his time better. He did care about their needs, and he was weary of living with his guard up.

In the morning, Dols described in detail his full

work schedule. No one exploded. There were definite disagreements about his priorities, but the discussion was thorough, appreciative, and constructive. He agreed to several immediate specific changes, and the vestry in turn agreed to help him review and organize his priorities. Beyond this, a new level of trust pervaded the room. In Bill Dols' words, "to a person, there was admiration and pride at participating together in some things that mattered." (Excerpted from a MATC newsletter).

Example 3

St. Mark's, Capitol Hill, is an old city church with a fifteen-year history of innovation. The pastor, Jim Adams, is in his early forties. A central value for Jim is lay inventiveness and lay control in both policy and program. He does not abdicate influence and exercises vigorous oversight. The church draws a significant portion of new members from people under 35 - rare for any church.

Each year the pastor and the lay leadership join in a retreat to plan new directions. An outside consultant is regularly employed to assist them design a good working session and to lend objectivity. Adams has said of these retreats, "They are painful occasions for all of us. I don't look forward to them. But each year we're grateful for the experience. It pays to look at what you've been doing, learn from it, revise and start afresh. So, the struggle is worth it."

On the first evening of a recent retreat, data on member wishes and reactions were presented for analysis and discussion. At the end of two hours of lively talk, the consultant, the Rev. William Swing, was asked for his impressions. He replied that during the evening a distinct picture had formed in his mind. "St. Mark's," he said, "is run and operated by an aging group of anti-institutionalists who seized power from the old guard ten years ago and now holds on to it jealously. From below you are being pressed by a group of enthusiastic younger members who want in on the action. Interestingly enough, none of that group is here at this conference. Why? Isn't it clear that by shutting them out you are in danger of losing the very values that you fought for? Values that still sustain this church and give it vitality?"

Adams recalled his own feelings at that moment:

The consultant's remarks were decisive. When he finished, I knew he was right. It was frightening to all of us. Certainly it was to me. I could lose truly talented people I had come to count on in exchange for younger aggressive strangers. I would have to build new relationships with a whole new group. It meant a new ball game for the church. I was afraid some of the older leaders would sulk off and leave for good. I wondered about my own influence - would I have as much and would it be the kind I like? But all of us felt a real excitement about what it could mean. We have had the experience of solving difficult challenges before. And I think we felt that if we dived in, we could find a way to make it work.

Some months later a parish planning conference was held at a large conference center. The invitation read, "If you want to have a hand in planning St. Mark's future, please come." Two hundred people did. It was, in part, a relaxed family time - drinks, recreation, and conversations. But each day there was hard, probing work - open meetings were held on every aspect of St. Mark's life - to hear ideas and formulate proposals to the vestry. Each evening, 'town hall' meetings listened and reacted to ideas. Following the conference, task forces continued to work on intensive planning and problem solving. In the end, a rich re-patterning of St. Mark's life took place. In some cases, power changed hands or was extended, a range of new policies and activities emerged, and essentially the community itself found rebirth. Jim's behavior was the key, his willingness to undergo the anxiety of a radical shift in his personal influence and his support to the board in risking congregational stability enabled them to find fresh reservoirs of energy and productive new directions.

There is, then, a direct correlation between a congregation's adaptiveness and a pastor's ability to provide integrative leadership.

The foregoing examples carry several implications:

1. The amount of influence in a congregation is not fixed so that as the members get more the leaders, by definition, have less. Intelligently shared, the amount of effective influence can actually increase, and with it the energy available for productive activity.

2. Facing anxiety goes against our natures, yet a high degree of stress naturally accompanies the pastors' work. Pastors must have a developed ability to monitor their own leadership anxiety and interpret its meaning - a sort of visceral radar screen hooked to an informed brain.

3. Each of us is a unique and limited person. Each has different things to offer and people respond to us in different ways. It is unreal to

expect pastors, or for them to expect themselves, to meet all needs. In reality, no pastor can effectively work with more than a few handfuls of people. The secret of evoking the talent and energies of a Christian community lies in creating networks of influence, not consolidating the power of one isolated individual.

Integrative influence requires a willingness to be open to the influence of others. It fosters in oneself the need to build one's sense of what is real, what is worth doing, with others, and to carry on the important and purposive acts of one's own life with them, rather than alone.

Frogs into Princes?

Can pastors shift their basic mode of influence? Can they, for example, change from reactive to integrative influence? Or, to phrase the same question differently, can pastors continue to develop autonomy and trust as they grow older? My own answer is, "Yes" - emphatically so - if the organizational settings in which they work are encouraging and, more importantly, if they want to.

From what I have said so far, it is obvious that the stance of the individual pastors toward leadership - their ability to face fear, act autonomously, feel compassion - is rooted in the structure of their personality. Personality theorists have, most people would agree, taught us to view the early and adolescent stages of life as the "formative years," so that when people reach young adulthood we think of them as no longer incorporating features of the world around themselves, but as "crystallized." The prevailing assumption about them and ourselves might be put this way: after 25 years we are finished products whose personalities are 'set.' We tend to believe that our ways of dealing with life at this stage are slated to be repetitive, and at best, susceptible only to small, limited changes.

In recent years, this view has shifted. Personality theorists, like Eric Erikson and Daniel Levinson, have begun to map out the life development of the adult personality. Erikson's own scheme, for example, lays out eight stages of life, and he emphasizes that we do not move through them in a regimented manner but in a continuous flowing process. While the adult years are still largely an uncharted, intriguing terrain, we have learned to know that adult personalities are open to growth, change, and new insight.

I do not imply that individuals must be models of trust, generativity, autonomy, and so forth before they can make it as pastors. Erikson's portrait, in fact, has a lot of room for the continuing development of autonomy and integrity at every point along the way. This is particularly so for individuals who, despite earlier adversity, are determined to put bad experiences to work for themselves rather than cave in to their constricting power. Such persons may never be free of self-doubt, dependent wishes, and anxiety, but they struggle through, despite them, to be 'alive,' initiating, productive persons. [4] Individuals are able to change the way they relate to the problems they have.

To take two minor examples from my own life. When I was in my later twenties my work began to require a degree of air travel and making speeches before large groups. Both were literally terrifying occasions for me. I avoided flying and took any way I could to side-step stating my views in large gatherings. As time passed, I became determined to master these fears. My strategy was simple - fly every chance I had and accept every reasonable opportunity to speak even if I collapsed (which never happened). Eventually, my terror softened, though to this day it remains palpable. Yet the point is simply that while both fears may always be there, I have altered the way I manage their power over my decisions.

The question is more than whether pastors can contrive to grow despite the limits of their nature. It is more than whether they can learn to use integrative forms of influence. The important question is, what will help them do so if they wish to. The answer, I believe, is found in two interrelated sets of factors: 1) an organizational set which tells us about the forces within the Church's life that influence pastors' personal development; 2) a personal set which tells us what choices and realizations within motivated pastors help them grow. I want to describe both sets in Chapters Seven and Eight. Up to now, the focus has been on defining the nature of leadership dilemmas within the churches. Now the question is, "What is required?"

7. *Acquiring Power to Lead:* Part I

For many clergy, difficulties in coping with the stress of parish leadership stem from the pastor's dependent status in the church. Thirty years ago, when there was a more solid consensus about the minister's role and the Church's purposes, the dependent position of the pastor was perhaps a less debilitating burden. The problem arises today, I think, because churches cannot sustain viability without leadership that is risk-taking, collaborative and vulnerable to change - precisely those constructive qualities of personal assertion that, under conditions of dependency, threaten the pastor's emotional and economic well-being.

For each of us, dependency and powerlessness are linked together. We are reluctant to take risks with whatever gives us bread and belonging. And if we look to the same source for our recognition and fulfillment as well, our reluctance to risk, to be vulnerable, is even greater. In exchange for these - fulfillment, recognition, belonging and food - we may (and often do) surrender autonomy and the ability to exert firm personal influence. Most of us have a great desire to conform and our inclination to risk fluctuates dramatically. It is usually easier to conform, and usually harder to assert one's own values and judgments in the face of misunderstanding and opposition.

It is a painful fact of life that, under conditions of stress, each surrender makes the next surrender a little easier, until a point is reached when one no longer has the power to assert one's deepest convictions and, indeed, may not even know what those deepest convictions are. It is ultimately possible to compromise away entirely, for the sake of security, one's capacity to act.

The elements of rapid social change and structural dependency now combine to make the question of influence a continuously problematic one for pastors. The more the

Church's environment changes, the greater the Church's need for thoughtful, challenging clergy leadership. The more their interventions rupture old perceptions and bring fresh perspectives, the higher the economic and emotional risks to pastors. They experience this crisis most acutely when they encounter significant gaps between the congregation's values and their own.

If systems theory is accepted, the response of every part of the Church (each system) to the crisis directly affects the response of every other part, ultimately affecting the response of the Church itself. It is essential that we grasp the extensive, interlocking nature of the pastors' problem of influence. By failing to do so, church leaders may grossly underestimate the complexity of the problems and the degree of patient hard work that must accompany intelligent efforts to revitalize the ministry.

Throughout these chapters I have maintained that a decisive factor in the Church's future viability is the ministers' ability, under difficult circumstances, to lead. I have tied this ability to such personal qualities as self-authenticity, an accurate knowledge of the dynamics of congregational leadership, the ability to share power, and the capacity to exercise informed choices about what leadership behavior best fits the circumstances of the parish at any given time. In all of this we have never been very far from another fact, namely that ministers cannot be isolated and treated apart from the organization and occupational settings in which they work, nor can the Church be viewed apart from the social environment in which it lives. There are, in short, other aspects of church life affecting the ministers' ability to offer firm companionate leadership during a revolutionary period of change. By examining briefly four such aspects - the selection of persons for the ministry, the judicatory reward system, the quality of support in the field after seminary, the placement of clergy - I want to highlight several important implications for all who are concerned with the vitality of the Church's ordained ministry.

Selection

During the remainder of this century, the quality of clergy leadership will be heavily influenced by the kind of men and women who enter the ministry during the next ten years. Leadership qualities of imagination, risk-taking, self-esteem, and flexibility are more easily developed if they are there to begin with. So from an organizational perspective, **who** the churches attract and admit as candidates for the ministry weighs almost as heavily as **what** the churches do to support and develop them as leaders once they are in and working.

In most denominations, judicatory leaders and seminary administrators guard the gates of entry into the Church's occupational system. Selection of persons for the ministry is more often than not a function of their personal judgments. Until recently, most denominations like my own chose ministers by **screening out** misfits rather than by selecting persons on the basis of desire, talents, and strengths. Churches have been historically non-interventionist with respect to 'recruiting' clergy leadership.

In the Episcopal Church, prevailing policy has been, and in many dioceses still is, to screen out applicants with obvious personality disorders or with weak educational backgrounds, accepting everyone else more or less on the assumption that either the seminaries, the Bishops, or the individual's congregation would take responsibility for refusing to recommend for ordination anyone who subsequently proved unfit. As Urban Holmes has observed, this amounts to an institutional practice of "screening by default," since once people enter seminary everyone involved tends to find it in their self-interest not to challenge their status unless they turn out to be publicly promiscuous, chronically drunk, or stupid.

Beginning in the early 1960s, clergy selection received more careful attention. In my own part of the Episcopal Church, we discovered that the moment we sought to recruit or to select applicants on the basis of specific strengths, a swarm of formidable problems suddenly descended around our heads. For example, suppose Judicatory Y decided that in order to be viable, churches must have ministers reasonably capable of constructive aggression and self-direction, open to collaborative relationships with laity; self-critical men and women with qualities of open-mindedness who, when necessary, could stand up against congregational norms. It may be fairly said that these qualities have not been regularly rewarded nor cultivated throughout the Church. Therefore, the number of applicants to Judicatory Y who exhibit these qualities or value them is apt to be small. So, at a fundamental level, the selection problem facing Judicatory Y or, for that matter, facing any church body where selection criteria differ markedly from those of the past, is that of effective recruitment.

If Judicatory Y decides to tackle recruitment head on and try to influence directly the quality of applicants to the ministry, a second problem appears hard on the heels of the first. Despite extensive behavioral science research, we still know little about how to identify accurately the presence in an individual of some of the qualities valued by Judicatory Y. Even more to the point, we cannot predict with reasonable certainty their appearance under the conditions of actual parish life. Judicatory Y, therefore, must hunch its way along, basing assessment of applicants for the ministry on the intuitive judgments of experienced clergy and laity.

Whatever methods it uses, Judicatory Y's commitment to make intelligent, discriminating judgments about the quality and growth of individuals preparing to be ministers requires a flow of valid information about their performance during seminary and in fieldwork settings.

Here again a palisade of problems rises up to block Judicatory Y's ability to evaluate and influence the men and women it sends along to seminary. Very real incongruities exist between the seminary world in which individuals prepare for parish leadership and the world of daily parish practice. In seminaries, faculty judgments about performance are traditionally formulated against academic and graduate school criteria, not necessarily the same criteria Judicatory Y has come to value. Moreover, the values and biases of individual clinical training and parish fieldwork supervisors are, as a rule, unknown to Judicatory Y leaders. The end result is that Judicatory Y's selection process must continually contend with a problematic flow of information, a hodge podge of facts and interpretations that is erratic, always incomplete, often beside the point, and inevitably flawed by subjectivity.

Beyond this, Judicatory Y has little hope under present conditions of exerting significant influence in the education and preparation of those it does select, for good or ill, to become pastors. There is considerable evidence that the seminary environment rapidly becomes the predominant influence in the development of a clergyperson's spiritual and professional identity.

This is an inevitable aspect of graduate, professional schools whatever the field. Under more ideal conditions, such a large proportion of seminary influence would be desirable. But given the lack of congruence between the realities of parish life and seminary education, Judicatory Y's low level of influence on the course of the theological preparation of candidates for the ministry is a serious matter.

The gap between seminary education and the parish ministry has haunted church leaders, laity, clergy and seminary faculty for almost two decades. It is a predicament, in my judgment, that the seminaries cannot correct by any of the normative prescriptions - relocating themselves on university campuses, revising curricula, setting up fieldwork programs - to name but three of the more promising. The basic problems in theological education arise from the fact that seminaries remain relatively uninformed by immediate, accurate, comprehensive knowledge of the leadership dilemmas of modern church life.

Unlike some graduate schools in law and medicine, seminaries still do not have the benefit of extensive interdisciplinary research into the actual conditions of parish practice. Candidates for the ministry for Judicatory Y learn most of what they learn in classroom settings still largely isolated from the human contexts in which their learning is to be used. This is not to advocate an expansion of the practical side of the traditional seminary curriculum. It is to emphasize the need for an integration of the functional, cognitive, and affective dimensions of theological education under conditions which closely approximate those of actual parish practice. Judicatory Y not only exerts a drop-in-the-bucket influence over its candidates, but it can anticipate receiving them back again after three years, educated somewhat in the scholarly aspects of Christianity, often with excellent person-oriented values, but ill-equipped and ill-prepared to contend with the turbulent demands of congregational leadership in a rapidly changing secularized society.

While the problems Judicatory Y faces are ultimately surmountable, they are complex and systemic. My point is not that one judicatory or even all judicatories in a denomination should dictate the terms of theological education, but rather that the power to affect change of every sub-system in the Church is limited or enhanced by every other sub-system. Similar scenarios could be written from the standpoint of seminaries or parishes themselves. The Church's long-term capacity to engender adaptiveness in its structures is influenced by the quality of the candidates it attracts, selects, and prepares in the next ten to fifteen years. At present, the tasks of effective recruitment and selection require patterns of innovative education, problem solving, value clarification, communication and coordination between judicatories, the professors, congregations and seminaries which we have yet to invent.

The Reward System

Another 'sub-system' of the Church that heavily influences clergypersons' capacities to respond to the dilemma of church leadership is the reward system of the denomination and judicatory in which they work. In every human organization, the reward system reflects the qualities and behaviors the organization values and honors with recognition and status. Ask a group of judicatory leaders (lay and clergy) to describe the prevailing picture of a 'good minister' in their denomination. Their replies will contain the salient features of their reward system. All clergy recognize and respond, at some level of awareness, to what constitutes 'success' as defined by their church.

In my own denomination, opportunities for recognition and status have been opportunities for managerial advancement. [1] According to the classic pattern, a 'successful' pastor moves along in a series of well-spaced moves, each time to a larger, more affluent congregation and then, ultimately, is elected Bishop. The question of how we adequately reward talented pastors who stop somewhere along the line is a basic question we have not yet resolved.

A common problem, for example, is that of middle-aged pastors of moderate or large-sized churches who are not Bishops and never will be. They have job tenure, are financially secure, are competent in one or more areas of ministry, run their churches in a sensitive, solid manner. Yet, as the years roll by, the only calls they receive are to similar churches in other cities, requiring them to pull up roots, break ties, really do the same job all over again. Despite their security, despite their knowledge, despite the contributions of their churches, despite the fact their congregations need and respect them, they become frustrated, bored, and sometimes apathetic. They function passably, but close to the bottom level of their energy and talent. Along with most organizations today, we have yet to solve the problem of how able ministers in mid and late career find fulfillment in jobs that are not at the top or even close to the top.

It is obvious that in any large organization, the vast majority of professionals cannot reach the top - in the Church, the great majority of ministers do not become Bishops. Yet, we have set the measure of recognition and status in proportion to advancement. There is a problem here that goes directly to the heart of the Church's viability as a social force. It has to do with the quality of ministry we reward.

There is a widely held belief among many pastors that innovative parish leadership is not highly prized within their judicatory. To a considerable extent, ministries of creative congregational development are likely to be rewarded with professional ostracism by peers and a mixture of suspicion plus respect-at-a-distance from church executives. Such ministries are viewed as problematic credentials for advancement and they are not accorded status. Whether this shared conviction among clergy corresponds to reality or not is a moot question; perception tends to govern behavior. We all know, or at least sense, that organizations receive the kind of leadership behavior they reward, or appear to reward. If qualities of innovativeness, self-development, autonomy go unrewarded, then one of three consequences are predictible for the Church:

   a) individuals possessing such qualities will not be recruited by the church;
   b) clergy will not be encouraged to develop and strengthen such qualities;
   c) clergy strongly valuing these qualities in themselves will remain on the Church's fringes as 'mavericks' or leave the ordained ministry entirely.

The **reward system** operating within a judicatory is therefore a critical element in fostering the evolution of a new style of parish leadership. To attract, cultivate, and support pastors capable of adaptive congregational leadership will require that church executives, and judicatory executives especially, shift their own values of ministry. In particular, there must be a shift that accords the aggressive development of the quality of congregational life a status equal to the production of growth and income. Specialized knowledge of leadership and sound innovation must be given a value equal to other kinds of managerial expertise.

To a great extent, church executives are administratively one or two layers removed from the congregational grass roots. While they do not escape the conflict and turbulence of the Church's life today, they are not as immediately vulnerable to economic and career sanctions within the occupational system of the Church. In comparison with pastors, they already possess a measure of independence which gives them a significant and promising degree of leverage in altering the judicatory's reward system.

An organization becomes unhealthy when preoccupation with promotion is more important to people than the achievement of the job they are in. [2] The point is that to remain adaptive, churches must learn to develop reward systems that give status to risk-taking, that honor the acquisition of knowledge, that give distinction to new forms of innovative congregational life. It means the invention of new ways to reward, not those clergy who avoid mistakes, but those who work collaboratively with laity to grapple with the disagreeable, exciting and complex opportunities of ministry today and evolve new

100

patterns of the Church's mission.

The Judicatory

The judicatory itself is a third key sub-system. In mainline churches, at least, the judicatory constitutes a primary sphere of influence for pastors because it has potential leverage in areas crucial to their well-being. By its action or inaction, a judicatory influences directly the placement and movement of pastors, the resources available for professional development, the types of technical assistance to congregations, clergy salary structures, peer relationships, training opportunities, and the very quality of the pastors' personal growth. Thus, there is a strong connection between clergypersons' ability to develop greater competence, greater self-authenticity, deeper fulfillment, and the organizational climate of the judicatory in which they work.

In my own two judicatories, we have concentrated on providing for young pastors settings where empathic and thoughtful reflection on work experience occurs with peers, congregational leaders and experienced professionals from other disciplines. One basic assumption behind this program, borne out by our experience, is that the pastors' capacity to direct the quality of their own professional life is linked directly with early experiences in which they learn to learn from others, to understand their strengths and limitations, to choose their values, and to articulate their own needs. A judicatory sensitive to this developmental character of the pastors' first year can do more than help new ministers survive, it can guide the basic direction of their early vocational life toward wholeness and integration.

This nutritive function of the judicatory with respect to pastors is a striking change from the past. In the traditional notion of a judicatory, pastors were assumed to be a stable organizational factor, requiring degrees of management control (depending on denominational polity) and little else. That ministers were also a leadership resource with needs of their own for continuing growth was not a rejected view, it was simply never considered, or at best only dimly perceived. Judicatories have been mainly guilty of neglect and unwitting policies of omission. Edgar Mills has reported that among clergy of twenty two Protestant denominations, 74 per cent reported they had no time designated by their congregations for continuing education and 80 per cent reported no money allowance for that purpose. [3]

Almost everyone has taken for granted that seminary (or some form of normative preparation) provided pastors with a once-and-for-all education for the ordained minis-

try. But this static view has begun to shift rapidly
under the impact of change and new knowledge. We already
sense that the great social events of the past fifty
years have created a new environment which constantly
changes for everyone. The traditional view of a one-time
education is being replaced in many professions and organizations by an understanding of the individual's education as a continuing process of learning and development
which under the best conditions is life-long and self-
initiated.

The evolution of this understanding, however, is
quite new in the churches. During the '50s and early
'60s, the attitudes of judicatory leaders about the post-
seminary requirements of clergy were dominated mainly by
two perspectives, the academic and the therapeutic. The
academic perspective favored role-related education for
clergy-training programs or university course work of
high cognitive input designed to strengthen the pastors'
ability to counsel, preach, teach, or administer. The
therapeutic perspective flourished chiefly in urban judicatories. By the late 1950s, sizeable communities of
psychoanalysts, therapists, and pastoral counselors had
gathered in metropolitan centers throughout the country.
These came to be sources of healing and growth, not only
for church members but for pastors as well.

In 1960, the Pastoral Institute of Washington reported that one third of its clients were parish clergy
seeking help "for job-related depression." Since then,
judicatory leaders with growing frequency have looked to
psychotherapy in some form as a preferred remedy for
clergy suffering from chronic role stress, marital
troubles, and vocational confusion. In 1970, for example, the General Convention of the Episcopal Church,
somewhat tardily, approved a denomination-wide health
insurance plan that provided 70 per cent coverage up to
$40,000 for outpatient psychotherapy for clergy and their
families.

During the 1960s, a third viewpoint emerged that may
be described as the **developmental** perspective. This
perspective grew from the contribution of psychoanalysis
and the applied behavioral sciences to our knowledge of
organizations and human growth. The developmental perspective had its specific genesis in the clinical pastoral education experience of thousands of clergy, the
human relations training movement, and the recent appli-
cations of organizational psychology to the problems of
religious institutions. Unlike the academic and the
therapeutic, this third perspective focuses on the interactions **between** the pastors and their organizational
surroundings (congregation, occupation, judicatory).

The developmental perspective has to do with three areas: 1) structural matters such as salaries; 2) personal needs of the pastor such as self-comprehension and purposive self-development; 3) moments of self-understanding, stress, or change that occur routinely in the day-to-day life of a network of churches. Figure 1, below, illustrates in graphic form basic developmental opportunities found in every judicatory and the type of innovative response judicatories in many parts of the country are already learning to make.

Figure 1

DEVELOPMENTAL MAP FOR JUDICATORY INTERVENTIONS

Developmental Point	Judicatory Response
ORGANIZATIONAL (Congregation)	
• Community change; serious internal tensions, inability to attract new folks; desire for innovative new directions.	Offers to broker organization , development consultation (potentially long term).
• Leadership change.	Offers consultant resources for parish self-evaluation, search and contract negotiation.
• Pastor's first year	Develops and offers model for pastor/board role negotiations; offers new pastors' program.
• New Board.	Offers consultant resources for value clarification and team building.

PERSONAL (Pastor)	
• Pastor's first year	Provides orientation to judicatory system and to community.

- First three years

  Provides program of guided reflection and peer support.

- Mid-life and pre-retirement years

  Offers to broker career assessment and life planning programs.

- Needs for increased self-knowledge

  Legitimates therapy and identifies first-class psychotherapeutic resources.

- Need for self-evaluation, performance assessment, and professional development

  Offers to assist self-reflection process; brokers resources for self-assessment with board; assists in continuing education planning.

- Needs for peer support

  Stimulates types of peer association to work on personal and ministry issues.

STRUCTURAL

- Salaries, housing, equity; medical and life insurance

  Develops and institutionalizes judicatory-wide policies and plan.

- Resources for continuing education and professional development

  Develops capital funds.

- Judicatory-supported congregation

  Provides consultation assistance to Pastor and Board.

More developmental points exist and remain to be discovered than Figure 1 depicts, but the chart does suggest the innovative potential of the judicatory.

There is, of course, in any expanded role of the judicatory a danger of the misuse of corporate power. The judicatory's dilemma is how to intervene effectively in the affairs of churches and pastors without subverting their independence, or increasing their sense of impot-

ence. We need relief from role conflict and ambiguity,
but not at the price of undercutting the integrity of the
local churches and their clergy.

What judicatories are faced with is the need to
search out new ways to assist pastors to increase their
power to collaborate and to take risks. Such explorations require an attitude among judicatory leaders that
is far from common in large organizations. It is the
rare wisdom to exert self-restraint on one's desire to
control from the top. It is a willingness to sacrifice
efficiency and control for the sake of evoking the creativity and resourcefulness of others.

Placement

A fourth sub-system clearly affects the pastors'
ability to master the pressures of structural dependency
- placement. Placement has to do with: a) the way
clergypersons move from one position to another, and b)
the manner in which they 'join up' with a congregation as
its pastor.

Religious bodies vary greatly in their ways of pla-
cing ministers. In some (Roman Catholic, Methodist)
clergy are **moved** by the church's hierarchy. In most
others, a clergyperson is invited (or 'called' by an
independent or nearly independent local church to be
their pastor). In either case, the degree of consultation
between the hierarchy, the church, and the pastor may be
minimal or extensive, depending upon the church's polity,
judicatory tradition and the inclination of the parties
themselves.

One critical placement issue, particularly in denominations where congregational independence is high, is
opportunity for movement. Under certain conditions, the
degree of opportunity for new work has a direct impact on
the quality of a pastor's leadership. In my own denomination, where the free market forces of supply and
demand tend to predominate, there has been a dramatic
shutting down of the degree of opportunity.

Over the past ten years, the number of Episcopal
congregations has increased only slightly - numbering now
around 7,500 - while the number of clergy has climbed to
nearly 13,000. A small percentage of these clergy are
non-parochial (chaplains, clergy about to retire, judicatory staff, seminary teachers) and do not compete for
the decreasing proportion of parish positions. This
group is easily counterbalanced, however, by another
factor - the impressively large number of churches scram-
bling to survive. About 40 per cent of all Episcopal
congregations have incomes of less than $25,000 a year.
Thus, they have only a marginal capacity to support a

full-time pastor and often pay considerably less than the Department of Labor's estimated minimal family income needs. (This situation is not confined to the Episcopal Church. In his study of clergy in twenty-one Protestant denominations, Edgar Mills found 84 per cent serving single churches with annual budgets of less than $20,000. [4]). Moreover, the figures for December 31, 1972 published by the deployment office of the Episcopal Church show 287 vacancies, of which only 56 were in parishes of 200-500 communicants, and only two in parishes of more than 500 communicants. A crude estimate of the supply-demand picture in the Episcopal Church would be: 4,500 viable parish jobs for 9,000 pastors, or two pastors for every position, with adequately-supported jobs opening up at a snail's pace.

A common example of the relationships between the quality of leadership and a restricted degree of job opportunity is that of pastors who have been in their present position six or eight years and are now ready for a new church. Pastors may want to move for one or more of a number of reasons:
- their personal, vocational, and career needs have shifted;
- they are not 'advancing,' and thus feel unmarketable, inadequate, not valued;
- the congregation's needs have changed;
- if close to 50, they are fearful of 'getting stuck' until they can retire at 65;
- they need more money;
- their relationships with the congregation have altered significantly.
Whatever the reason, they are aware of their own discontent and their slumping investment in the congregation.

Depending on their personal qualities and values, the pastors may decide to sit it out, or they will become active in their own behalf - preparing a resume, perhaps locating career guidance in some form, quietly getting out the word to selected clergy and friends, contacting judicatory officials. In the end, however, the result is the same should either strategy fail to bear fruit. If no church shows enough interest to call them, they become increasingly alienated from the institutional Church, increasingly unable to give themselves to others or to take risks, and eventually unwilling (or unable) to devote their energy and their talents to the creative tasks of leadership. If they are younger and inclined to be competitive, they may look for work outside the organized Church; if they are older, they may succumb to feelings of futility, withdrawing into bitterness or apathy while the congregation's energies begin to dry up.

The situation is further complicated by another placement issue - 'enjoined passivity.' Pastors who want to move have only a limited number of actions they can take. Despite greater knowledge of the tight placement market, prevailing norms in most denominations still discourage above-board congregation-hunting by clergy. This results in a kind of institutionally enforced power-lessness, putting clergy in the position of passive actors in their own future.

Pastors, if they are to respect themselves and sustain investment in the ministry, must not only find value in their job, they must also have the knowledge that new opportunities will be reasonably available to them, either through their own actions or those of the church.

A wise judicatory will try to soften the impact of a sluggish placement system. It will offer methods to help pastors and congregations remain sensitive and responsive to the changing needs of both. It will acquire up-to-date knowledge of vacant congregations (regionally and locally), broker interviews, challenge unproductive placement norms, and offer coaching in job negotiating to both pastors and churches. It will assist clergy in assessing their own talents and abilities so that they can better judge the best position for them. It will, in short, seek to increase the pastors' scope of self-directed autonomous influence over their vocational life.

*　　　*　　　*

Like Joseph's coat of many colors, large institutions are made up of highly differentiated parts. Within the Church, the four sub-systems I have described interconnect with still others: church executives, clergy associations, congregations, clergy families, seminaries, personnel policies, ideological viewpoints, support structures, and so on. Taken together, they constitute a powerful interwoven climate of institutional influence which acts dynamically to mold the quality of clergy leadership in local churches.

This very richness and complexity of life within most great institutions carries important implications for the modern dilemma of the clergyperson, and particularly for the question of clergy influence. First of all, the complexity of human sub-systems within the Church means that system-wide improvement in crucial areas is rarely, if ever, achieved rapidly or efficiently. This is true because these sub-systems **are interdependent with each other.**

Supposing a judicatory did manage to solve the recruitment riddle. That would be a praiseworthy achievement, yet it would carry next to no power to affect basic change in seminary education.

Suppose in the next decade or so seminaries begin to equip pastors to combat the pressures of dependency, give them basic tools for adaptive leadership and successfully imbue them with a deep respect for their own autonomy as human persons. That would be a magnificent accomplishment.

Yet, a countervailing denominational reward system could stifle these capacities within a dishearteningly short period of time, or force pastors themselves to leave the parish ministry for other types of work.

This point is plain: the power of any one sub-system is limited by its linkages with every other sub-system. For the churches, the net effect of this situation is that no one national church policy, no structural innovation by itself, no single judicatory program has sufficient comprehensiveness and impact to revitalize rapidly the ministry in a particular judicatory, let alone throughout an entire denomination.

Another aspect of institutional complexity appears paradoxical when set alongside the first - the interdependence of parts in a large institution means that one part is open to some degree to purposive influence by another part. With respect to efforts to resolve the crisis of clergy leadership, we have seen distinct advances. [5] For example, clergy associations have significantly upped judicatory salary levels and, in some dioceses, invented wholly fresh patterns of negotiating work agreements with congregations. Additionally, they have contributed to a fresh climate of mutuality among clergy. There is, moreover, a slowly increasing number of judicatories and national church offices which have started to provide money and programs for continuing education.

These features of large institutions carry, for me, another implication for the pastors' struggle to acquire power to lead. This implication holds particularly for those clergy who have the balance of their ministries ahead and for those entering the ministry during the next ten years. It is that **responsibility for rebuilding the pastors' power to lead (despite the conditions of their dependency) rests on the shoulders of the pastors themselves.** Clergy cannot wait for the necessary changes to be carried out by others.

There are obvious reasons why this is so. One factor is time - the rate of institutional improvements under the best of circumstances is painfully slow. Lasting changes in the conditions of ministry inside a jud-

108

icatory or denomination require the active cooperation, if not involvement, of ministers themselves. But if pastors passively accept their present plight, they prolong the impact of massive cultural and institutional pressures which beset most parish clergy and, predictably, intensify their own feelings of powerlessness.

There is an even more subtle problem here. The fact that a person has power over the quality of his vocational life is not to say he is either able, willing, or ready to use it. There is considerable evidence that many pastors are increasingly aware that structural dependence can stamp out identity, personal spontaneity, and creative leadership. Yet I cannot find any real evidence to show that pastors **in large numbers** have consciously begun to resist the impact of over-dependency. Growing numbers, yes; large numbers, no. Despite the flowering of clergy associations, despite new knowledge of clergy dilemmas among judicatory and national church leaders, my impression is that the number of pastors who remain passive or apathetic about the conditions of parish ministry far outweighs those for whom those conditions are a major concern.

This impression was confirmed when James Adams, formerly President of the Academy of Parish Clergy, told me that the Academy has consistently encountered widespread disinterest among clergy in any form of active personal and professional development. "The Academy, " Adams said, "attracts those clergy who, in a way, need it the least. They are already self-initiating, able to learn on their own, anxious to be more competent. Our question is, how do you arouse the vast majority for whom self-development apparently is not a value?"

It is naive, in one sense, to expect otherwise. In most professions, the number of persons who display a spontaneous concern for their own continuing learning and growth probably shakes down, along a bell-shaped curve, to between fifteen and twenty per cent. Also, the process of aging inevitably saps the motivation of others to continue to fight the battles of their youth or to resist vigorously negative aspects of their work. Among clergy there are those who consciously prefer the security of their dependent status in the Church. Still others would argue against the claim that self-autonomy and self-direction are important qualities in a pastor, believing that God requires a good pastor to be powerless and non-assertive. Challenging this belief is like challenging God.

Granting the presence of these factors, there is, I believe, a related psychological factor at work which contributes heavily to disinterest among clergy in their own growth as persons. For many of us who make our professional life within the Church, perhaps the most potent negative effect of structural dependence is to deaden the nerve of self-realization, to numb awareness of the impact of over-dependency and of our own power to act. I had a memorable experience of this process several years ago with a group of parish clergy.

The group had a good sampling of young as well as older, experienced clergy, all regarded as capable ministers, who were gathered for a series of meetings to identify obstacles to an effective ministry. Together we developed the following list of personal experiences as ministers where we had felt 'stifled' and ineffective:
- having to say "Yes" to every demand;
- fear of strong opposing viewpoints;
- appeasing aggressive women leaders;
- fear of feedback, finding out how I come across;
- not voicing needs for money;
- the need to appear busy;
- the need to be liked by everyone;
- inability the challenge parish values effectively;
- sitting on my values and convictions;
- inability to state my own job wishes clearly;
- lack of feedback, never knowing how I come across;
- inability to change any of these frustrations.

During subsequent meetings, the group searched behind these experiences, trying to learn the source of their stifling power from specific incidents that occurred in the course of each individual's day-to-day work.

As the pastors recounted incidents (one, for example, in which the pastor felt compelled to assent to a parishioner's demand, while feeling resentful and depressed at his response), we explored with them what they gained and what they lost by their actions. Often during these explorations, a critical moment was reached. This was usually when the pastors (and we with them) saw the self-destructive results of their behavior (their loss of self-esteem, their rage at feeling helpless, their lowered energy for work); or when they became aware of how much they wanted to be dependent and the price they were paying; or as they felt cold fear at the prospect of acting more in line with their convictions, despite the risk of disappointing or antagonizing a parishioner. At these times we felt considerable excitement and anxiety and, invariably, someone would abruptly puncture the tension by saying something like:
"Look, why the big deal; any job has its tough moments - right?"
"If we aren't prepared to sacrifice ourselves, we shouldn't have become ministers."

"That's life - you make compromises."
"You can't live without people - dependency is
necessary to living."
Any of these remarks could have been useful in other
settings. In our setting, at these moments, their effect
was to drain off the urgency of our feelings, obscuring
self-realization, and reasserting the 'unchangeable nature' of our positions as pastors; in sum, to block our
growth.

Why should someone want to stop the group's momentum
at these times? Because as potential moments of self-
awakening, they aroused anxiety. Consider what these
pastors were grappling with in themselves. As individuals became more aware of their feelings of resentment
and depression (or of their wishes to be strong and
creative) they also became more aware of the anxiety that
pushed them to deny the value of their own needs and
convictions. Like David, they began to realize how they
were traitors to themselves.

It is easy to understand why we often tend to dif-
fuse the power of these moments. One pastor described
the occupational and vocational life of the Church as a
"siren call" which lured him toward a refuge of "dream-
like security."

From these pastors I learned how often such attempts
to distract the group reflected a desire to heed the
siren call and preserve the refuge. "To some clergymen,"
one pastor said succinctly, "remaining depressed is pre-
ferable to the intensity of feelings that comes from
paying attention to your own feelings and experiences
with people." Ultimately, the support these pastors
found from each other gave them encouragement to press
through these anxious moments into a new sense of their
vocation. In September of last year, I received a letter
from a member of the group which is worth quoting in
part.

The experience enabled me to see myself as a
person distinct from the Church for the first time
since I left high school. I am starting to realize
in practice what I have the capacity to be. Before,
the Church was all I knew. I couldn't separate me
from being a priest. Didn't dare try. That's another world now. I feel a part of this congregation, but not 'of it;' equal to these folks, but
not superior or beholden in any way. I don't have
to have them in the church to live and I am a better
minister for it.

I have come to believe that for many clergy, acquiring power to bridge the value gaps within congregational life hinges on taking a first painful step into

awareness of the system-wide pressures which stifle autonomy and personal integrity. That is not the sum of it, but it is the beginning.

Autonomous clergy pose one obvious risk to church organizations. Some pastors will leave the Church. Some will experience the stir of new vocational promptings, ultimately deciding to move outside into other forms of work as a way of finding themselves.

But we must take the risk. It is the price of building conditions in which leadership can flourish. In this respect, churches and pastors are not unlike the elder brother in the story of the Prodigal Son - by not venturing forth, we remain secure, but at the cost of never enjoying our inheritance - more abundant lives of zest, depth, and meaning.

8. *Acquiring Power to Lead:* Part II

> Courage is a first step,
> but simply to bear the blow is not enough.
> Stoicism is courageous,
> but it is only a half way house on a long road.
> It is a shield permissible for a short time only.
> In the end, one has to discard shields
> and remain open and vulnerable.
> Otherwise, scar tissue will seal off the wound
> and no growth will follow.
> To grow, to be reborn,
> one must remain vulnerable - open to love,
> but also hideously open
> to the possibility of more suffering.
>
> Anne Morrow Lindbergh
> **The New York Times,** 3/1/73

In looking back over the experiences of pastors portrayed in these chapters, several important lessons stand out. The first lesson to be learned is that none of these pastors was familiar with the concept of leadership anxiety and its importance in day-to-day ministry. Few pastors have such knowledge. Seminaries do not teach it. Judicatories do not emphasize it. Pastors seldom talk to each other about it. Most clergy are left to their own devices to learn this critical dimension of pastoral leadership (if they do at all) by actual experience, usually at a high cost of severe emotional conflict to them and to their congregations.

The reader may remember David's remark, "I felt like a dead man." As a pastor, David possessed self insight; he did not underestimate his difficulty in loving others; he did not hide from himself his strong needs for control; and he accepted as inevitable in himself moments of duplicity and manipulation. Moreover, at a theoretical level, David knew that conflict was a predictable part of leadership and would tell you (accurately enough) that conflict was a disagreeable fact to be faced and worked through.

In a seminar or a classroom, David could speak impressively about the need for tension of spiritual growth if congregational life is to develop at all. Under the emotional stresses of leadership, however, David feared to disclose his feelings and perceptions openly (no matter how tactfully) on critical issues. Self-doubt and a growing sense of helplessness ate great chunks out of his self-esteem. Slowly, fear spread out into other areas of his work - contaminating his preaching, his energy for new programs, his enthusiasm, his heart for problem solving, and his ability to relate as an equal with the church's lay leaders. Ironically, David was in real danger of creating the predicament he dreaded most - becoming powerless to lead.

A striking parallel exists between the stresses experienced by parish pastors and those of a politician in a modern democratic state. Both are caught in the seething cauldron of hard choice - when to risk exceptional action and when to reflect popular sentiment.

A number of forces - structural dependency, the decline of their symbolic authority, the increased burden upon their personal capacities - combine to intensify stress for pastors in a manner akin to James T. Adam's observations on political life in the modern era. "As we look over the list of early leaders of the republic, Washington, Jefferson, John Adams, Hamilton and others, we discern that they were all men who insisted upon being themselves . . . . With each succeeding generation, the growing demand of the people that its elective officials shall not lead but merely register the popular will has steadily undermined the independence of those who derived their power from mutual election." [1]

The similarity between the pastor and the politician lies in the stress-creating climate in which they work. The seductive power of this climate is to make one believe "that security and advancement come only as one placates, appeases, seduces, or otherwise manages to manipulate the demanding and threatening elements in [his] constituency." [2] Under such circumstances, the decisive consideration, to paraphrase Walter Lippman, becomes not whether a proposition (or an idea, a value, a judgment, a hunch) is good but whether it is popular and acceptable.

In becoming free of one malady - autocratic pastors whose words carried the sacred aura of heaven's mandate - the Church may succumb to another equally fatal - walled-off pastors, armored against personal and organizational stress they do not adequately recognize. To be a pastor today is to confront complexity and therefore to experience anxiety. Health does not lie in the direction of ridding oneself of anxiety. Instead, anxiety is to be recognized, acknowledged, interpreted, brought into the light, befriended, accepted, used. When unrecognized and uninterpreted, anxiety will undermine the pastors' capacities to lead, and by a kind of domino effect weaken the congregations' ability to respond to the changing world within and around. David's mastery came, not as he rid himself of the anxiety of leadership, but as he discarded his shield against it. When he no longer used caution as an expedient defence (as other pastors might use hard confrontation), he could set his own convictions in creative tension with the normative values of the church members with far less deception or defensiveness.

There is another lesson which comes from the stories of pastors in this book. Nearly all began to change their leadership patterns as a result of discontent with themselves. Each felt an inner dissatisfaction that motivated them to learn. Some wanted to do better, to be more effective ministers; some were fighting chronic depression; others felt a floating, undifferentiated sense of vocational confusion and responded to a judicatory invitation to clarify their professional futures. Each was persistent enough to find another person, or a group, to assist him in analyzing his leadership values, pattern, and impact.

I believe the key for each pastor lay in the decision to examine his own leadership behavior **in the company of others.** Most of us, whether we are successful or not, have difficulty examining our leadership pattern. Breaking out of isolation, disclosing our own inner struggles, requires determination and courage few of us have. For these pastors, finding others to learn with became a way of supporting and strengthening their search for a better hold on themselves, first as individuals, and second, as parish leaders.

The problems facing most parish clergy in mainline churches today are so new, complex and swiftly changing that no extensive body of professional experience, precedent or knowledge about the modern practice of ministry exists. Images of ministry communicated through the medium of seminary culture are often twenty years removed from the realities of present-day leadership in the local church. Young pastors just entering the profession do not find a second and third generation of wise, older clergy around to supply them with the lore of the profession - reliable guidelines and clues for a vital practice of their calling.

Today's clergy are virtually thrown onto their own resources to pioneer and accumulate tested knowledge of effective congregational leadership in the turbulent environment of a modern, secular society. Pastors must learn to learn from one another, from each other's successes and failures, from each other's courage and risk-taking, from each other's fear and hesitance, from each other's vulnerability and inventiveness. The future of adaptive congregational leadership would thus seem to depend, in part, on the formation of small collegial communities of clergy, and clergy with laity. Out of these groups, in which experiences, support, critical judgment and learnings are exchanged, will evolve a widely accessible reservoir of knowledge about the nature of parish ministry today and tomorrow.

To sum up, an in-depth understanding about the nature of leadership stress, and an ability to examine their own leadership patterns in collegial groups, are both elements that modern pastors need in acquiring power to lead. But they are not sufficient by themselves.

There are, in my own judgment, specific perceptions of the self in relationship to the practice of congregational leadership without which companionate, risk-taking, vulnerable forms of behavior by pastors will not become organically a part of their personal style. These perceptions are, in simplest terms, learned self-realizations, recognitions that one comes to understand, grasp, and eventually affirm about oneself as a pastor.

In the remainder of this chapter I want to explore three such inner elements of the ministers' self-awareness. Each one enables a fuller sense of self and power to be; each makes possible a greater mastery of the anxiety of over-dependency; each increases the likelihood of relationships of shared power within the congregation.

1.   Moving into, Not Away from, Anxiety

In order to grasp this first realization, let us return once more to David and ask a question about him. What enabled David to survive, or perhaps more accurately, to regain his capacity to exert effective influence? The answer is that I think David did not like what he was becoming. David's change began at the precise moment "he came to himself," when he saw the consequences of his evasions for his work, his marriage and himself, and felt a sense of personal panic.

David had allowed his fear to drive him deeper and deeper into isolation until he was incapable of reaching out. He had good parish contacts and amicable relationships, to be sure, but they tended to receive increasingly lower investments of David's emotional energy and commitment. Without the life-giving sap of candor, these relationships become brittle and perfunctory. Rollo May states that "reaching out" to others is the basic meaning of aggression. It is to make "contact for affirmation of yourself and another or for hostile purposes, the way a bear hug is part of a pugilist's technique. The opposite of aggression is not loving peace - but isolation." [3]

David's avoidance of risk-taking on matters he felt to be substantive slowly rendered him allergic to his own aggression. In its constructive forms, May says that aggression includes such behavior as "cutting through barriers to initiate a relationship; confronting another without intent to hurt but with the intent to penetrate into his consciousness; warding off powers that threaten one's integrity; actualizing one's own self and one's own ideas in hostile environments." [4] It was in these terms that David perceived his power to influence as a man and as a minister rapidly draining away. Fortunately for him, self-disgust was not pure self-negation. David had a core of self-respect, both for himself and his talents. His discontent grew not from his failure to live up to an ideal role model of the priesthood, but from his awareness that his life was falling short of what it could be; living had become empty, flat and without savor. He was destroying himself and everything he cared about. It was in this spirit that he began to fight for himself.

The conversation with his wife led him to see that despite his fears and the risks of being forthright and vulnerable, the alternative of silence was worse. Recalling that period much later on, David described a picturesque half-humorous fantasy which occurred to him at the time.

> It was like I had been running blindly through dense underbrush, trying to escape. Suddenly, I burst out on the edge of a deep, roaring chasm spanned by a rickety half-rotten rope bridge, swaying in the wind and with no hand rails - no human being in his right mind would cross it. Except that coming after me was a herd of raging grizzly bears. I had to cross or die."

David did not alter his leadership pattern with an easy confidence that his Council or the congregation would be entranced at his emergence as a more forceful, clear pastor. Just the opposite. His decision to change was made despite his anxiety that people would find him objectionable and that, in fact, he would lose out to stronger minds and wills. David changed because he saw that evading the anxiety of his leadership position lit-

erally **cost him too much**, more than he wanted to pay.
Nearly all of his subsequent critical actions taken
during that period were accompanied by great nervousness
and anguish. Yet David persisted, and his triumph was
not a victory **over** the church or the Council, but **for**
himself.

In my experience, this courage in most clergy must
be learned. Mastering fear does not come naturally for
most of us, since our instinct is to move away from it.
But the common ingredient in the learning is the personal
moment of self-recognition when one becomes aware that
safety and security are not worth the cost. That insight
is to be seen elsewhere in Bill Dol's feeling that to
continue to hide would lead to "years filled with frantic
efforts and dishonesty." Anxiety faced loses its power
to deaden life and, in turn, bestows power to be asser-
tive, and yet vulnerable.

2. I Can Survive

The clergypersons' ability to acquire power to lead
is interwoven with their ability to act autonomously.
Essentially, this means possessing an inner confidence
that they can survive outside the Church, that they can
make it doing something else. However, within most of us
there is a constant struggle between autonomy and dependency. It is at this point that we are vulnerable to the
power of our organizations and they, in turn, vulnerable
to us.

Organizations may successfully appeal to our wishes
to be super-dependent in a degree destructive to the
general welfare. In the 1950s, a time of evolutionary
expansion within industry, William Whyte created the
metaphor of the "Organization Man" to describe this process in American business. In Whyte's view, modern business organizations successfully neutralized the individual good judgments of a generation of middle managers
by offering them a vast tranquilizing array of economic
and psychological benefits. In exchange for a future
without risk, these young men took on an organization-
fabricated identity as their own. Whyte foresaw a society of mega-organizations composed of manager drones, an
organizational "1984," "made in Detroit."

Whyte's vision of the organization clearly parallels
Dostoevsky's vision of ecclesiastical tyranny. In Ivan's
dream, the Grand Inquisitor tries to persuade Christ to
accept the single, great achievement of the Church
through the centuries. He says:

> We have corrected thy work and have founded it
> upon **mystery, miracle, and authority.** And men re-
> joiced that they were again led like sheep, and that

the terrible gift [of freedom] that had brought them such suffering, was at last lifted from their hearts. Were we right in teaching them this? . . . The most painful secrets of their conscience, all they will bring to us, and we shall have an answer for all. And they will be glad to believe our answer, for it will save them from the great anxiety and terrible agony they endure at present in making a free decision for themselves. [5]

The problem clearly is that, within such organizational settings as Whyte and Dostoevsky portray, our autonomous capacities soon atrophy from lack of use. If pastors surrender themselves completely to an occupational system that solves many basic life problems for them, they lose confidence in their ability to meet new problems successfully and with it, confidence that they can survive on their own.

A striking example of this was demonstrated during the life of a group of clergy with whom I met for a period of several months. One clergyman, Dan, had complained bitterly about the conservatism and niggardliness of his church members - he could not take a day off, the members would disapprove; he needed a secretary, the board would never justify the expense; people insisted he make house calls while he gave priority to other uses of his time, and so on.

At one meeting, the other clergy offered to help Dan work through a constructive approach to the matter of a secretary. Dan accepted. A plan was devised, and Dan stated his commitment to solving his problem. At the next meeting, Dan reported that he had been unable to put his plans into effect - circumstances had intervened, making it impossible for him to raise the issue with members of his church. Several weeks later, Dan again resumed his complaints. Suddenly, he was challenged by another pastor and asked whether or not he really wanted to change his situation. The exchange went like this:

Dan: People say that house calling is the most important thing I should do. They don't understand that four or five nights a week I have meetings. During the afternoons, half the homes are empty and the rest only wives and small children are home. What gripes me is that they think a clergyman has nothing to do with his time but ride around the city visiting empty houses.

S-: Dan, excuse me. I'm having trouble getting on board. A few weeks back, we worked on the secretary problem with you. At the time I guess I half accepted your explanation about why you could not ask your board for office help. But my impression

is you haven't raised the issue with them yet. Am I
right?

Dan: That's right. The agenda of the last meeting was
packed and I wanted to wait until I get a meeting
with a good piece of time to talk about it.

S-: Have you mentioned it to anyone else? For instance,
your Senior Board people? I mean, do they know how
strongly you feel about it?

Dan: They know I am concerned about it.

J-: Is it on the agenda now?

Dan: Not yet.

S-: That's my point. You don't seem very hungry to me.

J-: It looks like you'll let anything else get in the
way, like you really don't want to bring it up.

G-: Dan, you hear what these guys are saying to you.

Dan: That I prefer things the way they are?

G-: Could they be right?

Dan: I don't know. I certainly don't like things this
way. But I haven't acted hungry - I can see that.
That's a new thought.

B-: What do you think has gotten in your way? Is it
fear? For me it would be - I would say to myself -
people don't like pesky ministers, and back off.

J-: (Interrupting, to Dan) Let me ask you, do you feel
you can get a job with another church? You know,
are you marketable?

Dan: Well, I like to think I could find another
congregation. But jobs are really tight. If I get
fired from this one, word travels and I'd have a
tough time.

J-: How about another line of work?

Dan: Who is going to hire an ex-minister? You're locked
in.

J-: A department store. A school. A county government.

N-: I know Dan's feeling, though. Those are a whole new
way of life.

F-: Sure, so do I, but it sounds to me like Dan's the
one locking himself in. You've got your life
narrowed to two possibilities - this job or nothing.
You let it stay like that and those people will own
you body and soul! As long as you believe like that
you have no choice but to take all the crap. It's a
self-fulfilling expectation. And you end up
resenting them and hating yourself for being
helpless.

S-: That's right. Everybody's responsible for the crap
they take. Dan, you don't talk like you contribute
anything to your own problem. You blame the board,
the full agenda, the stubborn members - but isn't it
you who decides not to get your need for a secretary

squarely in front of the board? Isn't it you who decides not to push for it so it gets a hearing? True, you feel there isn't the money, that other things on the agenda are more important, but those are your decisions, not the board's. Nothing changes but it's because you decide to leave it alone. Until you see that, you can go on blaming these people and feeling helpless because they are your only hope.

Dan: Okay, that's true - I really don't push. It feels hopeless. I don't believe there is any use in pushing. These people are solid walls, they want the minister to be like a bellhop - available, ready, and no back talk.

F-: I accept the fact they're tough to work with. But you're not married to them, are you? I feel that until you start to push, you won't believe there is any use, and if you wait until you are sure of the outcome, you'll never start.

G-: Somebody else said it earlier, but I think Dan's got to work on the big picture - getting himself into a position jobwise where he **believes** he can make it no matter what. Maybe, Dan, you have to decide whether you want to stay dependent on one congregation and feeling lousy, or take the risk of doing something to begin to change all that.

Obviously, as long as Dan remained ultimately dependent for economic survival and pyschic nurture on the occupational and reward systems of the Church, he had insufficient will and self-esteem necessary to propel himself aggressively into two activities essential to the Church and his own spiritual health:

- the pursuit of congregational adaptiveness;
- the pursuit of his own continuing growth as a person and as a minister.

The issue of ultimate dependence is not only economic, it is richly connected to a range of psychic needs. In point of fact, for both Dan and David, economic factors counted less in their decisions than questions of value. Both men had to wrestle with what they ultimately prized in life, what they wanted for themselves, and the kind of persons they wanted to be. In the end, both had to face up to the meaning of their dependence upon the Church's system of rewards.

No one in the group expected Dan to become more autonomous in the twinkling of an eye, nor to flail out at his board in self-defeating attempts to "confront" and assert his power. The group pushed Dan to begin a journey into greater autonomy beginning **with one small act of self respect:** owning up to his own contributions to his situation. They perceived, accurately enough, that this required Dan's free acknowledgement that his helplessness was in a great measure self-imposed.

The struggle for autonomy carries its own liberating power. Paul Tillich emphasizes how the individual's power of self emerges in the struggle against aspects of life that negate and reduce being. To struggle, not against life, but for life is the essence of self-affirmation. How significant this struggle can be for both a pastor and a congregation is illustrated by part of an interview I had with a minister named Karl. Karl described his efforts to work out a depressing vocational dilemma that overtook him shortly after he turned 50, a point when churches often begin to bypass clergy in favor of younger men. Here is a portion of Karl's story:

Three years ago when I turned 50, I had been in my church about seven years. During that period, I had not received any calls to other churches. Most of the time, that fact didn't bother me much - it was true for most pastors I knew and I was pleased enough with the job. When I turned 50, though, all that began to change. The prospect of staying on in the same church another 15 years was depressing; also, I wanted a church with less of an administrative load but big enough to help me educate my three girls. Those things and the fact of no calls, pushed me into a depressing time. The whole thing seemed so big, too overwhelming to manage.

During this period I had a number of sessions with a career guidance man who had worked with another clergyman I knew. He began to break it down into small pieces for me. We talked about what I liked to do, what I was good at, what I wanted to do when I retired in fifteen years. I began to see that part of my dissatisfaction came because there were aspects of work in my present job that I hesitated to undertake since I didn't feel competent; and aspects I simply didn't enjoy much and didn't know how to avoid or pass them on. He helped me set up a plan for some advanced training; and suggested I talk over the other matters with the Church Council. I did both. Since then, I have taken night courses in adult education at the state university here in the county. Last year I began an intensive training program in family counseling. The fact is, I'm working harder and enjoying it more. I know I am laying a foundation for doing what I want when I retire.

Has it made me want to leave less? Well, everything is in a different perspective. Last week

I inquired about a state job in the Department of
Human Resources. Just to test my wings more than
anything else. I told them I wasn't out for the job
so much; I was interested in seeing whether this one
matched my needs. The interview was productive; I
learned a lot about them and agreed to return for
more talk. It's a good feeling of independence. I
find I am more committed to the people at the church
than I was three years ago. But at the same time, I
don't need them in the same way. They are not my
lifeline; I feel I can make it. It is interesting
how that makes it possible to like them better; to
be more understanding. If a call came, I would have
to give up a lot to leave.

Karl's decision to struggle against helplessness was
a liberating process for him. His determined pursuit of
self-respect and increasing competence acted like sun-
light on a plant. Karl came to realize he could survive
"without these people." That realization freed him to
trust and understand them, to work among them with far
greater self-affirmation. As he grew free to leave the
congregation, his decision to stay became less a matter
of external necessity, more of an inner choice willingly
made. Karl's redefinition of his pastoral relationship
with the congregation represented a small but actual step
toward mastery of his structural dependence.

For those clergy who sense their dependency is
greater than they want, it is important to know that
autonomy is like a muscle. It is not developed overnight, but by steady continuous effort. As in Karl's
case, there must be a commitment to work for oneself, a
pact with one's self-esteem to reduce the degree of
powerlessness over one's destiny in life. To gain the
realization that one can survive vocationally outside the
Church is also to acquire power to remain inside the
Church as a pastor of greater self-affirmation and personal force.

3. "The Church Makes a Lousy Mother"

For today's pastors, acquiring power to lead depends
on a third self-realization. The Church cannot be counted on to be a sensitive and wise employer for them.
Like every human organization that seeks to provide both
work and meaningful vocational expression for large numbers of people, the Church is a flawed, often insensitive, often coercive, often paternalistic organization
toward its principal employees - pastors and professional
church workers. The depth and keenness of this realization for pastors is critical since it connects directly
with their motivation to develop greater direction over

their own personal and professional life.

The drive for such power is the principal force behind the rapidly expanding clergy association movement. Since the late 1960s, increasing numbers of clergy have organized themselves in various types of associations (unions, senates, the Academy) to confront face-to-face problems of isolation, low income, vague professional standards, judicatory apathy, obsolete training, destructive personnel policies, and declining self-respect among ministers generally. These pastors' organizations are an interesting parallel to the nation-wide "rights" movement among minorities, women, prisoners, and consumers. Following the classical pattern of most organized attempts to counter injustice and to reduce burdens, a group of pastors tries to generate solidarity among themselves and enough collective power (using influence pressure rather than fiscal pressure) to improve church practices toward clergy.

A vigorous clergy association like my own (the Washington Episcopal Clergy Association) has one important psychological effect, among others, upon its members. It fosters a definite sense of distance, of independence, from the institutional Church. The presence of such psychological distance is essential for the pastors' deepening sense of autonomy. This experience makes it possible for pastors to feel less absorbed into the Church and therefore less helpless at the hands of their judicatory or congregations. Furthermore, the experience of distance makes it more difficult than before for them to be insensitive to their need for greater power to govern their own lives.

Distance also objectifies the Church for the pastors, etching its real flaws and real strengths in bolder relief, and stripping away some of its irrational aura as "benevolent," "unfeeling," "the Enemy," "omni-caring," or "undefiable." It enables clergy to spot the problems to go after, the abuses to correct, the key people to negotiate with, the strengths in the Church to reinforce. In sum, it shrinks the institution closer to life size and brings purposive change within the pastors' reach. In the face of an autocratic church regime, distance of this kind is required to resist exploitation and to preserve psychic strength.

At their vital best, clergy organizations nurture autonomy. But they are also vulnerable to the very real danger of a lapse into chronic preoccupation with a trade-union agenda - working conditions, salaries and benefits, and the deficiencies of management (Bishops, Church Executives, Lay Boards). As critical as these issues are for pastors, particularly within bureaucratic

124

forms of church polity, the organization suffers a failure of nerve when this lapse occurs. For it means that
the pastors' professional security within the occupational system of the Church has replaced their vocational
growth as its main purpose for being.

By far the most tenacious problem the clergy association movement must reckon with is not the clamor of
pastors for greater autonomy, but the ever-present wish
for security that is present among clergy as in other
human beings. Here again, we are faced with an aspect of
our dependent longing. It is the desire for a meaningful
existence that is free of fear. The strength of this
desire puts blinders on our eyes, shutting out its potentially harmful impact upon our relations with others and
upon ourselves. Just as structural dependence weakens
pastors' self-respect and undermines their inner freedom,
so does the wish for a safe, anxiety-free life blind them
to its consequences.

Strangely enough, the Church's need for compassionate, forceful clergy leadership runs afoul of its own
traditional practices as an employer. Security breeds
passivity. And passivity and risk-taking are mutually
exclusive, almost by definition. A pastor who does not
(for reasons of security) challenge the negative conditions under which he works, is not apt to challenge
effectively the same Church to face complex issues or to
examine its own life. Both go hand in hand. The link,
therefore, between pastors' willingness to let go security as their central operative value and the Church's
capacity to stimulate adaptive leadership is a clear and
direct one.

How do pastors learn to see their circle of safety
as, in fact, a self-imposed prison and decide to leave it
behind? That is a complicated question, psychologically
and organizationally. In my own work, I associate such
decisive events for pastors as flowing from a healthy
disenchantment with the Church. Depending on how a particular experience was interpreted and handled, disenchantment led to a sequence of events which culminated
when one of three things occurred: the pastors turned to
another kind of work; they retreated back into an even
more security-conscious existence; or they remained pastors, as more self-governing, integrated persons.

Perhaps the most recent, vivid recollection of this
process comes from the struggle of a friend to come to
terms with his disappointment in the Church's failure to
care for him as he had expected. At the time this happened, he was a staff member for a denominational office
in a city near Washington. For some time, he had felt
underpaid in comparison with other people holding roughly

similar jobs throughout his denomination. His particular position had been something of an organizational anomaly and there were no personnel guidelines to cover his salary. He decided to ask for a raise at his Board's annual budget meeting. My friend believed he had done competent work, and felt on excellent terms with his bosses. Therefore, without much hesitation he brought the matter up in a straightforward fashion. After considerable discussion, one of the members proposed a raise which he felt would clearly express the Board's strong appreciation. The motion quickly passed, and everyone turned and congratulated my friend. He sat there listening, he told me, in a state of shock. The increase was less than 20 percent of what he hoped for!

When he arrived home his anger was at a rolling boil. "Those cheap, ungrateful bastards!" he shouted to his wife. She listened and asked some questions. Had he asked for a specific increase? No. Had he presented any supporting material with his request - a list, comparing salary figures for similar positions, other precedents, or a suggested procedure for making the decision? No. "Well," she said, "looks to me like you've only yourself to blame. You didn't offer them anything to go on." It made him even angrier to admit she was right.

Later, still nursing smoldering feelings of injustice and betrayal, he went to a colleague and put the matter before him. The colleague listened for a long time. And then after a reflective pause, said to him, "Al, it's a painful way to learn, but now you know - the Church makes a lousy mother. You expect it to take care of you and you get disappointed, one way or another." For a day or so, my friend reflected. Both his wife and his colleague had been right. He had assumed the Church, these men who were his friends, would take care of him; he had handed over to them a responsibility they did not want and could not carry - that of being his parents. When they inevitably disappointed him, he became enraged and hurt.

He decided to go back to his Board, to make his request for a second time. But first he had to resolve a number of doubts and fears. Would not reopening the matter make him look ridiculous? Was not the lack of a coherent institutional policy about his job and that of many clergy subtly demeaning, a reflection of their true value when the chips were down? What if they hedged and said there was no money to meet his request? Or refused for some other reason? Or agreed to only half of what he asked? Would they permanently resent him for challenging the Church's hallowed norm - priests who care about money are selfish? Did he want to draw the lines of battle here? Was he prepared to resign and look for another job? Or was that simply another way of acting like a little boy? What if he had to negotiate? Could he do it? What was the most useful approach to take? Slowly and uneasily, he settled these matters for himself one by one. In the end, he went back despite his fears, this time better prepared. He came away from the meeting, with his raise, and with the feeling, he said, that for the first time in many years he was his own man. Al had broken out of the circle.

For me, what is important in Al's story is that not only did he come to understand the Church's indifference to his needs, but he began to take responsibility for himself. Al might have rejected the words of his wife and his colleague. Wishing to do business as usual, to keep secure and avoid stress, he could have turned his disappointment and anger inwards, and eventually become a dull hack at his work, deeply bitter about the Church. Or, he could have turned traitor against himself - simply by ignoring the value of his own needs, pretending they didn't matter or taking comfort in his good luck to have gotten any raise at all. Or, like an outraged child in a tantrum, he could have resigned without confronting the issue. His decision to go back had both the quality of mastering anxiety and affirming himself.

The fact that Al chose to stay within the Church is incidental to the decision to become "his own man." He might just as responsibly have decided to leave. The clue lies in his grasping, with a little help from his friends, what he was contributing to his own dilemma; that, plus a painful loss of illusion about the Church's indifference toward him. Al's disillusionment eventually mellowed into a kind of rueful wonderment, without rancor, that he could have been surprised at all. With autonomy goes the ability to acknowledge uncynically the imperfection of institutions, even the indifference of people to one's needs, and **at the same time** the ability to affirm one's needs, including the need for others, and the need to build better institutions.

4. Conclusion

In summary, then, these three self-realizations have a strengthening effect on pastors, increasing their power to lead. It is difficult to say which must come first in time: whether pastors first become disenchanted with the Church as caretaker and then develop the confidence they can survive; or, whether a growing sense of strength and skill gives courage to face anxiety and one's dependent desires, or whether mounting self discontent is required to get an accurate fix on the Church and develop one's own survival capabilities. Perhaps there is no special order for them to happen. In my own experience, they are continuous, interwoven and inseparable.

Their net effect is twofold. First, to make possible a sufficient separation between pastors and their congregations so that they can stand up against them, setting the tension necessary for growth. Second, to deepen pastors' consciousness of their self-respect and inner freedom to the point they can be allied with their congregations as friends and equals.

[handwritten margin notes: "I want to be / come somewhat from / being younger ... listen to my life story / show appreciation to compensate for / low self esteem / like myself best in life when / not like this"]

For a pastor to seek autonomy seriously means that he has settled a basic matter within himself. Namely, he has come to the point that he does not expect the Church to assume responsibility for his life and well being.

The search to be taken care of and the search for autonomy oppose one another. A recent conversation I had with a young clergyman illustrates this point very clearly. His boss, the senior pastor, had just accepted a position in another church, a situation which for a host of reasons left the younger man quite vulnerable. Here he was - inexperienced, less than six months out of seminary, with no tenure, no chance to succeed his old boss, in a semi-depressed economy, a tight church job market, no say about his new boss (who could, and easily might, ask him to leave) and facing a probable nine-month search for a new position.

"What arrangements do you have with the church about your future?" I asked.

"We haven't discussed it." He was honestly surprised.

"Do you plan to?"

"If there was a problem they would have said something, wouldn't they?"

"Can you count on them to look out for you that well?"

"Yes," he replied, "they are good people. They know how to run a church."

And, by implication, how to watch out for him. It's easy to sympathize. Under such circumstances, I know I would want to be taken care of. Certainly he may have sized up the leaders of that church to a tee. But that is beside the point. The point is that he was willing to hand over to someone else - the Board, the Bishop, perhaps God - the burden of deciding his future. Here, it is essential to note, the difficulty is not in the Church. Many of us would like to be taken care of. The difficulty is that this man **expected** his wish to be granted; in fact, counted on it, almost as a right. And moreover, he based his behavior on that expectation. Viewing reality in this fashion has a soothing consequence: it obscures the nature of his predicament, thus shielding him from anxiety. But it also has the potentially lethal effect of lulling him into a state of drowsiness, of complacent non-concern, of non-responsibility for his decisions - the antithesis of self-direction.

It is also important to emphasize the institutional roots of this young pastor's behavior. Few pastors are overly dependent for purely psychological reasons. Traditionally, churches have given substantial payoffs for over-dependence. Consider some of the more obvious: guaranteed status regardless of personal merit, freedom from responsibility for housing, salary, and the pastor's own job future, mediocre leadership tolerated in the name of Christian "love", the comfort of deferential, non-social relationships.

Why would any pastors give up such advantages to take on the anxiety of a more self-governing pattern of life? The answer is obvious. They want more from life and their ministry than over-dependence provides. That is, for whatever reasons, they want more authentic relationships, or greater congruence between their values and their behavior, or to be more forceful leaders, or simply to be 'their own person,' however defined. In exchange, they will bear the heightened stress and do the psychological work involved. But until the cost of remaining over-dependent exceeds the cost of self-direction or, conversely, the advantages of autonomy become irresistible, a pastor's commitment to self-direction is likely to be thin.

As we have discussed earlier, autonomy is not a socially isolated state of being. It does not mean doing your own thing as a pastor, imposing on the laity your vision of the Church, being a law unto yourself. Nor is autonomy spiritual solipsism, a self-complacent humanism closed to the presence of grace and the reality of other people. For clergy it is, among other things, the capacity for inner self-direction in the company of others whom they are called to serve, the ability to hold in tension a clear sense of their own primary needs and the primary needs of the community, coupled with a commitment to share power in concert. Autonomy leads to more, not less, openness in relation to the laity. Given the whirlpool of forces besetting clergy today, they must have as a matter of course the inner capacity to act under stress and to withstand considerable loneliness,

130

and the willingness to push steadily for interdependent relationships with laity in pursuit of the Church's mission.

There are, in my judgment, three promising paths for pastors toward greater autonomy.

First, by gaining greater independence within the Church's world of work, thereby reducing their sense of psychic captivity within the institution.

Second, by acquiring competence as authentic guides into the Christian life for a congregation.

Third, by developing the capacity for sustained personal growth under the pressures of parish leadership.

For today's pastors, these core elements are central to the realization of firm leadership under stress. Each carries the individual pastor in two directions at once - toward solidifying inner resources and toward greater solidarity with others in the congregation and the community.

In the remaining parts of this final chapter, I want to explore each in turn.

I.   Independence in the Church's Work World

Why do pastors need greater independence as far as their work is concerned?

There are at least two answers. Integrative leadership (blending their vision and talents with those of other people) is all but impossible for pastors as long as they feel locked into their current jobs. As long as their current jobs appear essential for survival or fulfillment, they simply will not take the necessary risks or tolerate tensions of leadership. That is the psychological answer.

Occupational turbulence (e.g., the oversupply of clergy, the growing use of part-time clergy) makes the search for fulfilling parish work problematic for nearly every pastor. That is the organizational answer.

Both answers fit into a wider view as well: clergy are buffeted by the same social forces that affect everyone else. Wherever we look today there is the impact of occupational dislocation: once-productive lines of work (autoworkers, stockbrokers, house builders) are vulnerable to depression overnight; the Bureau of Labor statistics report that four of five Americans change occupations at least once in their lives. Such examples can be multiplied nearly ad infinitum. But they mean that for the foreseeable future, most of us must learn to cope with a rapidly changing world of work. Clergy cannot survive spiritually or economically on old habits. They must form new attitudes about how to search for the right kind of work, and even how to support themselves through alternative forms of non-parish work.

A Passive Tradition [1]

Until recently the old ways worked well enough. During the years I was rector of St. John's Church, Oxon Hill (1958-65), I talked regularly with a nearby colleague, Roland Jones. We would share news, advice, encouragement. Every now and then one of us would ask the other, "Had any calls?" * Tense moments. Invariably, when Roland answered no (as both of us always did, except once or twice), I felt simultaneously relieved and uneasy - relieved that Roland had not received a call while I, like a plain girl at the dance, had been passed by, and uneasy about the possibility the system might not work for me a second time. Like most Episcopal clergy, Roland and I unwittingly accepted a number of maxims that ruled the way we looked at work in the Church. In reality, they amount to little more than magical thinking. Maxims like:

- Trust the invisible and silent workings of the Holy Spirit; your next position will appear at the right time, which is God's time.
- Church executives were your allies - trust them (if the Spirit was tardy) to find you a job.
- Ordination is for life, once a minister always a minister. (Thoughts of alternative careers seldom dawned. The ministry had no honorable exit).
- When ready to move, don't openly advertise. Discreetly inform tested friends and activate the old-boy system in your behalf. (Advertising indicated that somehow the system wasn't working for you - you were damaged goods).
- Don't approach a vacant church and ask to interview: too much chutzpah or the Christian equivalent.

Where work was concerned, the old ways taught childish dependence. The institutional message was plain as a steeple: work hard, rock no boats, shine brightly, and wait to be found. Because they didn't need to, clergy seldom honed their abilities to search for new work, few seriously considered alternative careers, few learned to renegotiate their work when they grew restless and longed for fresh challenges.

Today, a number of factors have eroded these venerable traditions. One: the clergy surplus forces all

---

* Among Episcopal clergy in those days, a "call" was a loose colloquialism for both the offer of a new position or an overture from a seriously interested congregation.

but a few prestigious pastors to compete in a market where only the fittest survive. Two: church executives are learning the wisdom of recommending pastors, not because the individuals need to move, as in the old days, but because their qualifications fit the Church's needs. Three: to an alarming extent, clergy who want to move can't or don't or won't - they stay in churches long after they should have left - increasingly apathetic, distracted or resentful. Perhaps most importantly: many clergy have come to recognize that, in fact, they are essentially alone in the Church's occupational system. Peers are competitors; denominational offices are set up to serve the parishes, not the pastors; church executives understandably enough want to protect their own turf by screening out mediocre clergy.

So, the new message is also plain: to remain authentically invested and spiritually alive at work, most pastors must cut themselves loose from the old maxims. That is, however lonely and unsettling the prospect, it is better to do something else with your life than endure the cost of empty work. Cutting loose also means learning how to influence the conditions of your work as a parish pastor - what you do and where you do it.

Becoming Active

Let's examine both in turn. Other than by inheriting or marrying wealth, how do pastors know they can survive outside the Church? Clergy I know for whom that conviction is solid came to it by different routes. Some, like Karl, literally trained themselves into independence: they studied, learned new skills, pursued their own professional development, until one day they felt able to test the water and discover they were marketable in another kind of work that appealed to them. Thus, they had at least a genuine choice to remain where they were, or to act out their ministries in a different setting. A rare few I know were blessed with enough natural self-confidence and talent to believe instinctively that they could take care of themselves under any circumstances. For the rest, there was no single script, except the facts of hard personal struggle, spurred by knowledge of their own vulnerability and their need to grow. As a result, they arrived at a place where personal fulfillment no longer depended upon the institution or the good opinion of their parishioners and church superiors. These pastors are not callous. What they have is the hard-won inner knowledge that, if necessary, they can stand alone and do what's necessary to survive.

About the second aspect of cutting loose from the maxims of the past - finding and negotiating new work - I want to make a number of specific observations. Learning to find a new position and to reshape the nature of your ministry demands fresh attitudes and behavior.

1. The old maxims implied that the initiative was out of your hands. The current situation demands an attitude toward work that keeps the initiative in your hands. Pastors must act as if they were without human resources of any kind in this world, except those they identify and organize on their own behalf. That's obviously not true, of course, but they must learn to act as though it were true.

2. In most mainline denominations, job placement resources (a clergy deployment office) are not organized primarily to help you but to help the employers - parishes and church executives. For example, most judicatory personnel offices are there to screen out weak clergy applicants, not to help you find work. So, learn to use such resources, but never count on them.

3. Bart Lloyd of the Mid Atlantic Career Center (MACC) offers a perceptive observation: "If you want to leave the parish position you are in, the first thing to do is stop looking for a job. It's more important to get the right job, than any job. The right job uses your talents and skills." The starting place, then, is self-knowledge.

4. In brief, you need to get an accurate fix on:
   - your abilities (what you do best) and values;
   - your personal and family needs at this stage of your life;
   - the kinds of parish needs and problems that turn you on.

5. A parish job is more than a vacancy created by somebody else's resignation. In reality, it is a cluster of unique, unmet congregational needs. Matching your abilities and needs with the right set of church needs is your critical task. That requires self-knowledge.

6. It also requires a strategy. In denominations like my own, where hierarchical control fluctuates widely, diocese to diocese, clergy move into new positions by personal influence, and chiefly by ability to use networks of personal communication. In my diocese, the majority of new pastors were first recommended to search committees by a respected clergyperson or lay leader. A strategy aims at putting together your own network of people willing and able to help you.

7. The target of any strategy is to be interviewed by those Boards, church executives with power to

hire you for work that uses your abilities, in a
location pleasing to you and your family, at an
appropriate salary under conditions favorable to
your personal development. So you must:
   a. Find out how each judicatory you are interested
       in handles placement: the policies, procedures,
       and chief actors.
   b. Form a list of people you can call regularly by
       telephone to keep abreast of positions as they
       come open.
   c. Wherever possible, interview those in a position
       to help your search and recommend you for inter-
       views, e.g., judicatory staff people, church
       officials, for positions that look right for you.
8. So far, the best book I have seen on resumes and
    interviews, two tricky areas, is Richard Lathrop's
    Who's Hiring Who. [2]
9. Perhaps the most important ingredient in a healthy
    pastor-church relationship is the mutual ability to
    clarify regularly what they want from each other,
    identifying core areas for growth and development.
    In reality, pastors and churches instinctively re-
    sist the candor and work necessary to these impor-
    tant exchanges. Where such a climate exists, it has
    been consciously built out of the knowledge that
    expectations constantly shift as the congregation's
    internal and external environment changes, as new
    lay leadership replaces old, and as the pastor
    ripens in the job. That is why it is important to
    talk explicitly during the contracting period about
    evaluation. Satisfaction and effectiveness are tied
    directly to being able to influence and realize the
    priorities of your work. From the beginning, build
    an expectation of periodic feedback and re-negoti-
    ation between yourself and the Board.
10. In searching for work, obviously your position is
    strongest when you don't have to have the job for
    which you are interviewing. Desperation makes bad
    judges of us all. So, develop a sense of anticip-
    ation - start to look for work before you have to.
11. Consider Richard Bolles' epigram, "Getting a job is
    a job in itself." Cutting loose from a heritage of
    passivity where work is concerned requires time,
    research, self-reflection, planning, and the stamina
    of a long-distance runner.
    To sum up, pastors are virtually powerless to com-
fort or challenge others, whatever their job, if they are
convinced that they cannot survive outside the Church, if
they believe that they cannot find work when they are
ready, and if they feel that they cannot change or in-

fluence the shape of their daily work.

The foregoing, both conceptually and practically, fosters personal influence over the circumstances of their work. As a result, by increasing their freedom to find work outside the Church or different work within the Church, pastors firmly increase their freedom to review repeatedly their commitment to the job they have.

II. Acquiring Competence

"Sometimes pastors feel like they're trying to eat with boxing gloves: they've got no way to handle things they need to get at." [Paul Barrington, Pastor, Central Baptist Church, Little Rock, Arkansas]

In most things, competency generates self-esteem and a sense of personal independence. This is particularly true where work is concerned. In our society, individual identity and worth are tied psychologically to success in the market place. This is so in more than material terms. It extends to how others value what you do and how well (in your eyes, in theirs) you do what you do. That is why there is a direct relationship between a pastor's competency and his or her independence.

Despite the tremendous gains of the last five years made through continuing education programs, clergy associations, and church-wide concern about clergy training, the question of competency remains a profoundly troubling one for pastors and the Church as a whole. We are still plagued by four major happenings that helped fuel the ministry crisis to begin with: psychotherapists and behavioral science practitioners took over traditional areas of pastoral care; basic shifts in our views of reality undercut traditional images of God, casting doubt on the basic worth of the pastor's message; clergy were ill-prepared for the stunning variety of values and ideology that have emerged in society; and concepts of parish leadership taught by seminaries lost their applicability.

Out of the resulting crises grew a vigorous concern among clergy for professionalism that concentrated on the acquisition of skills and cultivation of effectiveness. This search has been, in part, a quest for a new definition of the minister's craft, a fresh synthesis of new knowledge and new skills. But it has also been part of something much bigger and far less tangible - the need for a contemporary vision of the pastor's role that knowledge and skill can express. And that search is far from finished.

Over the past ten years, a clear trend has emerged in ministry development. Clergy have generally sought greater professionalism through the doorway of role-

136

specialization - singling out a traditional clergy role (counselor, liturgist, preacher, manager) that feels congenial and learning to do it with extra special skill. The purpose of this behavior is plain. It is hoped that amidst the blizzard of demands that beset pastors, they will be able to find the stability and reward attached to doing one important thing very well.

Role-specialization, I have come to believe, is a misguided way to look for authentic competency or to recover the lost vision of the pastor's work. Why? Because role-expertise does not get to the heart of the dilemma. That dilemma arises because the social context in which any or all of the traditional roles of the priest are carried out has drastically altered.

While great numbers of people seek religious experience, the old religious practices are no longer spiritually and psychologically effective for them. In this situation, beefing up skills as a pastoral counselor or social-action leader **by itself** has a real but seriously limiting value. It will, in reality, create the illusion of related professional growth while simultaneously distancing pastors from their basic apostolic leadership. To achieve authentic competency today (both in fact and personal conviction), pastors must shift their attention away from specialization and toward an altogether different arena. They must learn to focus on the struggles of their people to be more fully human. The aim and purpose of Christ's ministry was that human beings may live more abundantly. If we, as pastors, are seriously concerned to make possible for modern people that quality of liberated life promised in the Gospel, then we must acquire a new competency that cuts across any traditional role of the pastor - the vision and skill to search and assist others in their struggle to find wholeness and to work for wholeness in society.

From my vantage point, this is exactly what laity crave from clergy. I regularly participate in meetings in which laity and clergy talk over their expectations of each other. Time and again, the principal theme of these conversations is the need for clergy to devote their principal energies to spiritual leadership. Obviously, behind such a popular cliché are deeper, but related wishes. These wishes are definable, I believe, in the following terms: to conquer fear arising from the persistent and often insurmountable problems life presents, to have one's religious heritage come to life, to experience with some depth the reality of mystery and awe, to experience God. Beneath everything, the essential yearning articulated in these meetings is to be capable of recognizing and experiencing meaning to life in oneself.

If I were a parish clergyperson at the point of deciding the future direction of my ministry, I would seek ways of becoming an effective guide into the Christian life for a congregation. Here the word "seek" is apt. As yet, clergy and lay leaders do not have the knowledge and tools that show us what form this guidance must take. The territory remains to be charted. We must invent directly from our experience, capture from other traditions, and rediscover from our own. But, I believe the first step in acquiring authentic competence lies in accepting that challenge.

Fortunately, there are solid clues for where to start.

First: we must start within the individual, not within tradition itself. That reverses the normal order. Routinely, clergy are trained to tell others the meaning of life by proclaiming to them the Gospel or teaching them Christian doctrine. Ira Progoff is entirely correct in pointing out that this kind of communication no longer works for large numbers of men and women, because we have so little common community of discourse in which ultimate questions of life can be discussed. That is why, as Progoff has written somewhere, to achieve "the new atmosphere of awareness our time requires, we have to refer not to doctrines or beliefs, but to facts of experience, to inward events as modern persons can know them." That means learning to address ourselves to the subjectivity of the individual in a particular way: at the points where each of us struggles with the threatening experiences of life and seeks to be related meaningfully to others. At this level, meaning cannot be explained or pointed out, it has to be discovered.

Second: we need to be clear that there are specific life experiences that bear directly on the realization of a more humane existence. What I refer to are those experiences of selfhood that are at the core of every individual life and of life in society: growing up and separating from parents, forging an identity, becoming a parent and raising children, achieving and failing to achieve one's ambitions, finding and expressing one's talents, acting out citizenship, finding community, living with war/depression/catastrophe, physical illness, working out one's sexuality, aging, widow[er]hood, grief, dying, and throughout all the changes of life, maintaining a sense of meaningful self-hood.

These experiences are common to most of us. Their religious character comes from their power to push us to seek new depths of awareness, to find new integration, to redefine ourselves and our relationships with others. Each threatens because it goes to our primal core, dis-

138

these people who are experiencing intense moments of this?

times to touch base w/ others theme —

are there preaching

rupting normal patterns, threatening us with chaos and loss, arousing anxiety, opening possibilities for new growth. Each sets life beyond our direct personal control and invites us into a healthy state of dependency with others. By learning to touch the inner life of persons during the course of these experiences, we learn to reach through to the place where the search for meaning is alive.

Another clue, a critical one for clergy: specialized methods are required. We must have methods that assist people explore the depth dimensions of their lives in personal and social terms. Here again the traditional methods of teaching clergy in seminary do not work. They depend largely upon exegesis, explanation and information giving, always assuming particular doctrines and beliefs. Both proclamation and symbol are present in the worship and educational life of every church. But if clergy are to become useful guides to others, they must learn to open up the deeper levels of human experience where life is under the pressure of growth or disintegration. They must learn methods of education and explanation that do not depend upon a traditional pedagogy or assume a specific set of beliefs. In particular, clergy need to have:

   a. methods of deepening self-awareness, e.g., guided personal reflection, life story telling, meditation – so that individuals may explore their own inner space and the primary content of their past and future lives as social beings.
   b. methods for group work in which people share and explore common experiences and events central to life and develop sensitivity to the levels of meaning contained in their own religious tradition. (Excellent examples of these methods are found in Washington-area churches which have used and adopted the curricula of the Educational Research Center in St. Louis, Missouri).
   c. methods by which the congregation becomes conscious of the meaning of its internal interactions and its external relationships with the world around. In particular, focusing upon the degree of interdependence existing between clergy and laity, upon the nature of the congregation's response to the struggles of the community, upon the capacity of parish leaders and members to challenge effectively the folk religion operative within the congregation.

These methods root the pastor firmly in the apostolic functions of ministry. To build competency through role-specialization is to emphasize subsidiary or secondary aspects of the pastor's work and to risk profess-

ional irrelevance. If this happens, it would be sadly
ironic, since the search for a new professionalism among
clergy was started originally by pastors who correctly
sensed how vapid much parish life had become and how much
personal effort was needed if pastors were to recover the
art of congregational leadership.

Certainly the evolution of a specialized competence
as guides into the Christian life for congregations could
well revitalize the ministry. That is obviously to be
hoped for. But to anyone who has personally felt and
engaged in the struggle to be a competent pastor during
the past twenty years, it offers another possibility. To
those who accept the disciplined search, there is the
hope of working once again at the ancient core of the
pastor's role and, together with that, recovering both
one's distinctive contribution to the tasks of the **laos**
and the energy for the complex professional demands of
parish leadership.

III. Sustaining Personal Growth

To sustain the capacity for personal growth, pract-
icing ministers need constantly to balance opposing ten-
dencies within themselves, and between themselves and
their congregations. These opposites are basic to their
role. They are continually caught, for example, in at
least three fundamental tensions: the tension between
comforting and confronting, between controlling and sharing control with others, between encouraging healthy
dependence and stimulating growth toward interdependence.

Significantly, a pastor's basic medium of leadership
and action within these tensions is his or her own person. Character is as critical for the minister as skill-
ed hands for the brain surgeon. Obviously, there are
other essential elements - a sound theological education,
leadership skills, a good placement, to name several.
But character is the key. To address a congregation on a
controversial matter, to accept gracefully one's own
personal limits and not be sucked into the draining cycle
of saying yes to every human demand, to be with termin-
ally ill persons, to help a hesitant church council face
painful disagreements, to invite feedback, these are not
only acts of skill, they are personal acts of character.
They depend upon a degree of self-liking, accurate self-
knowledge under the conditions of stress, a sense of
ultimate vulnerability, a touch of toughness, and a willingness to communicate one's deepest feelings to others.
That is why it is destructive nonsense to teach pastors,
as the Church has often done, to devaluate the force of
their own personalities. Cultivating and putting to use
their internal resources as individuals is the challenge

faced by all pastors.

Probably a commitment to personal growth has always been demanded of clergy. And it is good to remind ourselves of how this is also true today. In many churches, the ascendent definitions of a good pastor and a good church often fly squarely in the face of values of spiritual growth and social concern. Rather, they reflect productive norms (bigger budget, member increase) necessary for survival and favored generally by society. In this kind of church atmosphere, concern for the personal struggles of individuals and social justice are not absent so much as dormant, peripheral.

Conventional parish values frequently downgrade these aspects of reality, cutting people off from their own life experience and from each other. Pastors, of course, can succumb to these forces as readily as anyone, with the same result - a growing poverty of inwardness. Every pastor knows what this feels like and learns to recognize the symptoms in the parish: the compulsion to work endless hours, the inability to meditate, pray, read, the deadening of passions, vulnerability to theological fads, vagueness about one's own frame of reference as a Christian. Possibly "busy-ness" and its by-products are a form of materialism that fills a vacuum inside many of us. An old clergy colleague, Charles Kean, once observed about pastors, "when you've made the machine run and the whistles blow, at least you know you've done something! Hoopla is its own satisfaction." In any event, resisting such pressures requires disciplined personal power. The pastors whose integrative leadership was illustrated in Chapter 6 showed a measure of this kind of inner strength, acting competently under pressure, speaking with a minimum of defensiveness, standing against authority out of conviction rather than rebellion, challenging without rancor the prevailing dependency of their congregations.

The situation today poses an important question: what conditions make for personal growth in any person whose full-time work is parish leadership? Lay leaders and judicatory executives might find reasons to wonder if personal growth is possible at all for clergy. Pastors themselves need to have an accurate sense of what specifically will assist their growth. Let's look at this question from two different but related viewpoints, a) the pastor in the context of the congregation, b) the pastor in relation to himself, herself.

There is, I believe, an important link between pastors' capacity to grow and their refusal to become isolated in the course of parish life. In the literature on clergy distress (emotional breakdown, physical collapse, forced exodus from the ministry, job hopping, alcoholism, promiscuity), personal isolation consistently appears as a big factor. Being out of touch with and unable to influence lay leaders is a more negative element for pastors than the experience of stress itself. In fact, becoming isolated under the conditions of prolonged stress is a predictable prelude to a collapsed ministry.

The opposite of isolation is not intimacy nor even conflict-free cooperation. It is rather a commitment, certainly on the part of the pastor, to work together in a climate of mutual respect for differences, particularly differences about the religious purposes of the Church and the pastor's role. Stress in these areas must be taken for granted but while the stress is inevitable, the outcome is not. The toxic consequences of extended stress do not occur for pastors who are open to conversation and feedback (formal and informal) about the effects of their leadership on the church.

For their own sustenance as leaders, pastors must work to build up primary groups of persons in which such talk goes on and from which they can derive accurate perceptions of themselves in relation to others. If they are not committed to such groups, no one else is likely to be. If such groups do not materialize within the first year or so on the job, pastors will lack the raw materials to establish firm, effective leadership within the congregation. It is essential to emphasize that as a result everyone will handle stress badly, usually by glossing over significant differences or falling into unproductive, persistent squabbling.

The experience of the Rev. Martin Townsend offers an example of this building process at work. Early in 1974, our diocesan Commission on Ministry asked me to carry out a pilot project in clergy performance evaluation. The Commission was disenchanted with the various schemes of performance assessment used by other denominations and proposed by our National Church. In our judgment, they tended to adopt a reward-punishment psychology that intensified the conforming pressures on the pastors and generally took for granted that pastors were to subordinate themselves to the parish's purposes, leaving little room for the development of their individual strengths and goals. Thus they lacked the power to motivate personal growth and learning, something we felt was basic to any process of clergy evaluation.

On the other hand, the Commission recognized the crucial relationship between the pastors' effectiveness and an informed picture of how they were doing "on the job." Tested, dependable knowledge on generating such pictures was lacking in our diocese.

142

Together with a small group of interested clergy, I prepared a proposal which was presented to the Washington Episcopal Clergy Association in May of that year. Our aim was to learn how to help ministers evaluate their work productively. There was general agreement that the pilot project should:

- legitimate questions individual pastors were actually asking about their work, such as: how do I come across? how can we clarify what we expect of each other? how can I develop more interdependent relationships within the Church?
- put control for the evaluation directly in the pastors' hands: they decide, finally, what information they need, from whom, and who they need to help them interpret it.
- focus on the pastors' interactions within the congregation.
- OK the pastors' ownership of the information, e.g., they decide if the judicatory office gets a copy.
- assist the pastors to specify what actions they intend to take as a result: changes in leadership behavior, in work priorities, in time management or in new plans for continuing education.
- create a wider base of lay persons able and motivated to talk candidly with the pastors about their shared interactions and their common ministry.

We indicated that the project would be tailored to the specific concerns of each participant. From our side, I promised consultant resources, a degree of objectivity and personal experience in helping church boards and pastors talk through what they require of each other. A capable colleague of mine, Roy Oswald, had agreed to join me, so the project had the benefit of two staff people. In response to our offer, eight clergy, including Martin, signed on.

Martin Townsend was rector of St. Christopher's Church, Lanham, a two-hundred member, predominantly white middle-class church east of Washington, close to the Beltway. He had been there four years. During the first meeting of the project group, we concentrated on finding out the evaluation needs of each person. Martin indicated that he wished to find out a) how he was doing in his ministry; b) a clearer picture of what was expected of him; c) what was negotiable.

His aims, Martin told us, were eventually to get a salary increase, plan his continuing education, check for a need to shift his time priorities and negotiate support for areas of his work that he felt were weak. He wanted to involve his Vestry and committee chairpersons, about 25 people in all. Martin assumed that these people had pertinent information and views on these questions. But he believed, as we did, that it was highly unlikely they would volunteer this material or were even readily conscious of it. He felt that each should be interviewed, in depth and separately. To increase the objectivity of these interviews, Roy and I suggested Martin invite three lay persons from another church to conduct the interviews. Martin readily agreed. He also agreed to identify areas of his leadership for which he wanted feedback. Roy Oswald agreed to meet with all the participants to go over the plan and secure their cooperation. The hardest part, we anticipated, would be developing a sound approach to the actual interviews. We looked forward to exploring the results with Martin and the participants as the meat of it, the most exciting part.

Something occurred almost right away during Roy's evening with the Vestry which is worth noting. It became apparent that great confusion existed in everyone's minds about why Martin wanted feedback. Whose idea was it? Was it for contract or salary changes? Was it for Martin's own growth? Roy and I had agreed from the start that evaluation for purposes of personal growth should be disconnected from salary negotiations. It invited game playing from everyone. That was Roy's position, initially opposed by Martin himself. In the end, it was agreed that St. Christopher's would develop other procedures to set Martin's salary. The interviews were solely for his personal development and theirs.

Subsequently, during September, the interviews were done. Martin, Roy and the interviewers collated the material and highlighted areas of interest. Then in early October, Roy led an extended meeting with the Vestry, committee heads, and Martin.

Because of the wealth of material, Roy asked everyone to focus on specific areas of conflicting data related to Martin's preaching, the balance between his organizational and spiritual leadership, and his use of time. The talk explored feelings, probed assumptions about roles, supported Martin's wish to strengthen himself, searched for new understandings. As a result of the evening and of his reflections in the days afterward, Martin decided upon a number of shifts in his behavior which he shared with the people. The longer-term changes bore up well, and were still in practice a year later.

- In response to the wish that he emphasize the spiritual dimension of his work, Martin enrolled in workshops and conferences that focused on new methods of enabling people to explore and develop their own spiritual life.
- Martin and the Vestry decided the attention to cer-

tain administrative matters should shift from his
shoulders to theirs.
- He would spend a regular part of each day in meditation, reading and personal reflection.
- He would spend more relaxed time each day with his
family.
- Martin sat down with the parish commissions on worship and adult education to go over carefully the
purpose of each sermon at the two main services and
discussed appropriate changes in his role and style
as a preacher. He arranged for regular feedback
over a period of time.
Talking with Martin later, I found several of his
own reflections on the process to be particularly illum-
inating.

I had to believe that there was something positive here for me to do this. It's pretty scary. I
had to trust the people who were getting the information. I knew outsiders wouldn't screw me. Also,
I had the veto power throughout, that was important.
The results were a surprise to me. I do really have
more time with my family and it's improved my relationship with my wife. But the biggest surprise
came when I started getting positive feedback (which
I wanted, of course); I was struck by how much I
craved it. It made me feel terrifically vulnerable,
and I could see myself giving in to it. It taught
me I needed authenticity in myself and to be less
defined by others. What started as an evaluation
really put me into my own journey as a person. It
fed my soul.
Martin's story illustrates a number of conditions
which nourish pastors' personal growth:
1. The presence of a group which gives valid information about the interactions between pastor and
congregation that affirm the pastor's strengths and
is critical in important areas.
2. The pastors' own control of the process and a clear
sense of what they want from it. If they can determine the depth and scope of the inquiry so that it
conforms to their need to know that both their level
of trust and their incentive to hear will be sufficiently in balance to permit lasting insights.
3. The pastors' internal commitment to getting this
information is an indispensable ingredient. Without
it, there is no energy or momentum to do the considerable work involved and to take the risks of
pushing into painful areas.
4. The emergence of personal development and/or work
goals that reflect the values and needs of the

pastors.

5. A clear pathway to achieving those goals and a sense of support from the people who count.
6. The presence of a third party, an outsider, whose competence and objectivity are trusted. A consultant of this kind can probe, challenge, surface new areas, question assumptions, straighten out communication, supply needed skills, and keep the tension of the process at a productive level.
7. A group of laity - at least some of whom are in key positions - who have pushed through their fear of talking "straight" with a clergyperson about what they want from him or her, what they are getting, and how they are prepared to help.

+ Anne Miller
+ Committee
+ Board?.

The Pastor in Relation to Himself, Herself

Chris Argyris maintains that there are three ingredients which make possible the expression of competence and personal effectiveness in individuals, regardless of the nature of their work. [3]

- Self-acceptance: the degree to which the individual has confidence in himself or herself. The more individuals value themselves, the more they tend to value others.
- Confirmation: when others experience me as I experience myself, that is, when I am able to gauge accurately the effect of my behavior on others.
- Essentiality: the more I am able to use my central abilities and express my central needs, the greater will be my feelings of essentiality to myself and to the setting involved, e.g., work, family, community.

Where pastors are concerned, I would add a fourth: realistic self-knowledge under the conditions of parish leadership. The more pastors learn about themselves, amidst the routine encounters in church and community, the less likely they are to act blindly under the power of people's unhealthy dependencies and their own personal needs. And, of course, the more of themselves they have to share with others.

This requires self-knowledge in critical areas. Knowledge particularly about: how to use their own anxiety constructively, their needs for closeness and their relationship to their leadership style, their characteristic uses of power, the way they view the minister's authority, how they tend to manage differences between themselves and others. By gaining such knowledge, pastors increase the range of leadership behavior available to them from situation to situation.

In my own experience, there are two ways clergy may

enhance their degree of self-acceptance, confirmation, essentiality and self-knowledge as parish leaders. The first is by means of competently guided peer groups devoted to professional development.

Clergy professional development groups have mushroomed in recent years. These should not be confused with conventional colleague groups of the kind recommended by the Academy of Parish Clergy. Colleague groups often provide good support, but little lasting development. They generally lack both the security and the kind of effective confrontation necessary for personal growth. A number of features distinguish a good professional development setting.

- There is at least one consultant/guide trained in theology and the human sciences.
- The main focus is on the person and role of the pastor amidst the actual dilemmas encountered in ministry.
- There is a basic concern to provide accurate knowledge of the forces at work between the pastor and the congregation.
- There is commitment to deepening each participant's awareness of his/her own religious traditions.
- There is close attention to each individual's strengths and the personal obstacles that block his or her effectiveness as a pastor.

Some examples: The Pastoral Counseling and Consultation Center's (Washington, D.C.) two-year training program taught by Charles Jaekle for clergy couples learning to do parish-based marriage education; Intermet Seminary's professional development seminars; some short-term programs at the Institute of Advanced Pastoral Studies at Cranbrook; seminars in our own diocesan Intern Program; the Metropolitan Ecumenical Training Center's orientation program for new Washington clergy.

Genuine personal change can be easily over-estimated in these groups. No one group does it all; each has different assumptions about the pastor's role; each reflects the peculiarities of its leadership and group composition. But above all, such settings are simply in a primitive stage of evolution, probably like the state of aviation in 1910. We are in the Spad and de Havilland era of clergy development.

Nevertheless, they do have power to enable growth.

First, because they offer peer solidarity, a community of fellow learners. To the participant, this comes in the form of "I am not alone, or at fault," a sense that the complexities of the parish are objective facts, not the result of personal inadequacy. Second, there is a commitment to hard work and a conviction that personal change is possible. Third, these groups provide core knowledge about the work situation of pastors and what they can do to improve the quality of their ministries.

A second way pastors grow personally is through psychotherapy. Many church people will view this statement as troubling, perhaps absurd. It even troubles me, for reasons I shall cite in a moment. But first, let's consider the aims common to most psychotherapeutic methods, despite differences in basic philosophical schools: the increase of self-esteem, the integration of one's past with the here and now, a liberation of gifts, the ability to face and bear anxiety, greater vulnerability to risk in personal relationships, and less need to control tightly the world around. In every respect, these elements are essential to the character pastors require to do the specific task of congregational leadership. Viewed this way, psychotherapy is far more an educational process for pastors than a medical remedy.

What troubles me about psychotherapy is its lack of general applicability. In my experience, its effective power for pastors is limited by the fact that so many circumstances must be "right." First and foremost is the desire of the pastors to change and grow - they must **want** the experience because they are dissatisfied with themselves. Otherwise, therapy in any form will not take, no matter how warranted it may appear to the individual's friends and associates. Secondly, in therapy what heals is the quality of the relationship with the therapist. In groups, it is the quality of interactions among the members. This is far more important than the quantitative volume of insights acquired in the process. Finding the right interpersonal mix at best is a tenuous matter composed of hard searching and good fortune. Then there is the cost. Psychotherapy at the rate of once a week has a per year cost roughly equal to a year in college. For most clergy salaries, that is out of reach. Some denominations like my own have insurance coverage for a major portion of therapy fees, up to a designated total. But that practice is far from widespread.

Finally, geography is a limiting factor. Psychotherapy is still largely an urban phenomenon. To have a chance at the best therapists, you have to live close by a large urban area. For these reasons, psychotherapy is not likely to be the pathway toward personal growth of even a majority of motivated pastors. Nonetheless, when the factors are right, psychotherapy can make the essential difference between a ministry of manners dominated by unhealthy fears and unrecognized needs, and a ministry of deep and authentic personal power. In other words, psychotherapy is not a substitute for God's healing power; it is a process through which one becomes more open to the active presence of Grace.

A Concluding Note

The mainline churches are in transition now. Many of us, laity and clergy, are still caught up in the old images and practices of ministry. Still, it is clear that new patterns already press in upon us. In my denomination, as in other parts of the Church, the coming years will likely see a diminution of the pre-eminence of the priesthood and a new awakening of the laity. That's all to the good. But in a way it's not the point. The point has to do with life itself, and how we live it. "To be alive is to be pained," writes Colman McCarthy. For each of us the point is how to live with dignity and fullness despite the pain and changes life brings. Without people to share it with, without courage to be vulnerable, and without compassion, life is empty. That is what Judaism speaks about; that is what is plainly shown us in Jesus as the Christ. The Church, as a living community, must express that truth in words and deeds.

In pushing toward a redefinition of ministry, clarity about how a community renews the spirit of compassion within itself is essential. That clarity is supplied by Jesus in His refusal to avoid the anxiety of caring and retreating into indifference, by His vulnerability to rejection at the risk of caring, and by His final dependence upon nothing finite. What His story reveals is true equally for clergy and laity, regardless of their different roles and functions in the Church. So, no matter how we reshape the Church's ministry if the result fails to express in viable terms what makes the pain of life bearable, it won't count for much. And if we, in some measure, become more compassionate, less self-deceived, more accountable to the suffering around us, we will have more than enough energy and courage for the transition years ahead.

FOOTNOTES

Chapter 1
1. In a striking passage, Ernest Becker describes the same aspect of our natures. **The Denial of Death.** New York: Free Press, 1973, p.187.

Chapter 2
1. **The Washington Post.** Sunday, August 24, 1975.
2. Ibid.
3. Bennis, W.G. and Thomas, J.M., **Management of Change and Conflict.** England: Penguin Books, 1972, p.12.
4. MacMurray, John, **Freedom in the Modern World.** London: Faber and Faber, 1932, 1938, p.27.
5. Luckman, Thomas, **The Invisible Religion.** New York: Macmillan and Co., 1976, pp.104-105.
6. **The Washington Post.** May 13, 1976.
7. MacMurray, John, op. cit., p.58.

Chapter 3
1. Graham, Aelred, **Contemplative Christianity.** New York: Seabury Press, 1974, p.79.
2. Letter to St. Mark's Congregation, by the Rev. James Adams, winter, 1972.
3. Graham, Aelred, op. cit., p.11.
4. See Jean Haldane's **Religious Pilgrimage,** an Alban Institute Publication, 1974. While interviewing members at St. Columba's Church, Washington, D.C., about the nature and course of their own religious development, Mrs. Haldane found that none of her respondents perceived the church as interested in their own individual spiritual growth nor expected guidance, help or encouragement from the church in this respect. In varying ways, each person saw the church as primarily concerned with the "socialization" of members into its own particular purposes.

Chapter 4
1. May, Rollo, **Power and Innocence.** New York: W.W. Norton and Co., 1972, p.100.
2. Ibid.
3. Robinson, J.A.T., **Exploration Into God.** Stanford,CA: Stanford University Press, 1967, p.39.
4. This small model was adapted from a planning scheme developed by Educational Systems Designs, Westport, CT.
5. Kung, Hans, **Why Priests?** London: The Fontana Library of Theology and Philosophy, 1972, p.36.

6. I am indebted to the writings of Bruno Bettelheim, particularly **The Informed Heart,** for my original realization of the importance of autonomy for pastors and for the definition I give to it throughout.
7. Ibid.
8. This point is clearly elaborated by Edgar W. Mills in an unpublished article, "The Intentional Minister," 1972, p.13.

Chapter 5
1. Fletcher, John C., **Religious Authenticity in the Clergy.** Washington, D.C.: An Alban Institute Paper, 1975, pp.1-2. Inter/Met was an experiment in congregationally-based theological education that closed in June, 1977.
2. MacMurray, John, op. cit., p.164.
3. Ibid. p.60. I am indebted to John MacMurray for the distinction between "average human life" - life as it is intended to be, "not mastered by fear" - and "normal human life" which for the most part is bound up in anxiety.
4. Fletcher, John C., op. cit., p.5.
5. Ibid. p.6.
6. Jud, Gerald J., et al, **Ex-Pastors.** Philadelphia, PA: United Church Press, 1970, p.73.
7. Ibid. p.76.
8. Ibid. p.76.

Chapter 6
1. The four major strategies are adopted from a theory of leadership developed by Educational Systems Design, Westport, CT.
2. Arendt, Hannah, **The Human Condition.** New York: Doubleday Anchor Books, 1959, p.179.
3. Educational Systems Design, Inc., **Building Open Systems.** p.7.
4. Hodgeson, Richard C., et al, **The Executive Role Constellation.** Boston: Harvard University, Division of Research, Graduate School of Business Administration, 1965, p.36.

Chapter 7
1. I am indebted here to Peter F. Drucker's useful and provocative discussion of status and advancement in modern organizations, **Landmarks of Tomorrow.** New York: Harper and Row, 1965, pp.83-89.
2. Ibid, p.93.
3. Mills, Edgar, **Continuing Education and Occupational Stress Among Clergy.** Ministry Studies Board, 1972, p.5.

4. Ibid, p.18.
5. Bittsburger, Donald E., "Crisis in Ministry: Is It Healing Itself?" **Leaven**, Vol.14, Number 17, 1975.

Chapter 8
1. Adams, James T., **The Adams Family.** 1930, p.95.
2. Lippmann, Walter, **The Public Philosophy.** Little, Brown and Co. (Canada), 1955, p.27.
3. May, Rollo, op. cit., p.150.
4. Ibid, p.151.
5. Dostoevsky, Fyodor, **The Grand Inquisitor.** Association Press, 1948, pp. 27, 31.

Chapter 9
1. Much of the material in this section first appeared in an article I wrote, "The Minister Looks for a Job," (Washington, D.C.: The Alban Institute, 1974) and then as a chapter titled "Getting a Job" in John Biersdorf's **Creating an Intentional Ministry.** (Nashville, TN: Abingdon Press, 1976).
2. Lathrop, Richard, **Who's Hiring Who?** Englewood Cliffs, NJ: Prentice Hall, Reston Publishing Co., 1976.
3. Argyris, Chris, **Intervention, Theory and Method.** Reading, MA: Addison Wesley Publishing Co., 1970, p.39.